KT-474-971

Pocket
STOCKHOLM

TOP SIGHTS • LOCAL LIFE • MADE EASY

Becky Ohlsen

In This Book

QuickStart Guide

Your keys to understanding the city – we help you decide what to do and how to do it

Need to Know
Tips for a smooth trip

Neighbourhoods
What's where

Explore Stockholm

The best things to see and do, neighbourhood by neighbourhood

Top Sights
Make the most of your visit

Local Life
The insider's city

The Best of Stockholm

The city's highlights in handy lists to help you plan

Best Walks
See the city on foot

Stockholm's Best...
The best experiences

Survival Guide

Tips and tricks for a seamless, hassle-free city experience

Getting Around
Travel like a local

Essential Information
Including where to stay

Our selection of the city's best places to eat, drink and experience:

◎ **Sights**

✖ **Eating**

🍷 **Drinking**

✪ **Entertainment**

🔒 **Shopping**

These symbols give you the vital information for each listing:

✆ Telephone Numbers	👭 Family-Friendly
⊙ Opening Hours	🐾 Pet-Friendly
Ⓟ Parking	🚌 Bus
⊘ Nonsmoking	🚢 Ferry
@ Internet Access	Ⓜ Metro
🛜 Wi-Fi Access	Ⓢ Subway
🍃 Vegetarian Selection	🚋 Tram
📖 English-Language Menu	🚆 Train

Find each listing quickly on maps for each neighbourhood:

Bar Hemingway

16 🍷 Map p233, B2

Legend has it that Hemi
self, wielding a machine
orate this timber-pan
ered bar during
showpiece is a
en by Papa ar
town. Dress
s.com; Hôtel Rit
⊙6.30pm-2a

Lonely Planet's Stockholm

Lonely Planet Pocket Guides are designed to get you straight to the heart of the city.

Inside you'll find all the must-see sights, plus tips to make your visit to each one really memorable. We've split the city into easy-to-navigate neighbourhoods and provided clear maps so you'll find your way around with ease. Our expert authors have searched out the best of the city: walks, food, nightlife and shopping, to name a few. Because you want to explore, our 'Local Life' pages will take you to some of the most exciting areas to experience the real Stockholm.

And of course you'll find all the practical tips you need for a smooth trip: itineraries for short visits, how to get around, and how much to tip the guy who serves you a drink at the end of a long day's exploration.

It's your guarantee of a really great experience.

Our Promise

You can trust our travel infor-mation because Lonely Planet authors visit the places we write about, each and every edition. We never accept freebies for positive coverage, so you can rely on us to tell it like it is.

The Best of Stockholm 125

Stockholm's Best Walks

Stockholm's Best...

Survival Guide 145

QuickStart Guide

Welcome to Stockholm

Sweden's stylish capital is an accessible beauty, easy to navigate and gorgeous from all angles. Its old town, Gamla Stan, is a saffron-and-spice vision from the history books, while the modern city centre rewards cool-hunters and food fanatics alike. Outside of town, royal palaces loom over lakes, and tiny red cottages decorate windswept islands.

Gamla Stan (p22)
DESEO / GETTY IMAGES ©

Stockholm
Top Sights

Skansen (p52)

Known as 'Sweden in miniature', Skansen is an open-air museum and park that serves as Stockholm's communal playground. It's home to a Nordic zoo, historic buildings, a glassblowers' hut, live-music performances and lots more.

Vasamuseet (p56)

This wildly popular museum was purpose-built to tell the story of the short maiden voyage and long restoration of the massive warship *Vasa*, which sank to the bottom of the sea within minutes of setting sail.

Kungliga Slottet (p24)

Stockholm's imposing royal palace – the world's largest still used for its original purpose – houses some beautiful examples of Swedish baroque and rococo interiors. Guided tours make Swedish history entertaining.

Stockholm Archipelago (p120)

A scenic boat ride among the thousands of rocky islands in the Stockholm archipelago is one of the loveliest ways to relax on a summer day. Have some extra time? Kick it up a notch and stay overnight!

Drottningholm
(p108)

The excellent guided tours of the Renaissance-inspired summer palace bring generations of Swedish royals vividly to life, and the parklike setting couldn't be prettier. In summer, go by boat to get the full impact of the place.

Millesgården (p96)

The former home and studio of beloved sculptor Carl Milles is a work of art in its own right, with its elaborate Italianate house, modern gallery and beautiful outdoor sculpture garden.

Historiska Museet
(p84)

An utterly engrossing place, this museum spans 10,000 years of Swedish history, using artifacts and multimedia installations to re-create the Viking era, show off pillaged treasure and illustrate medieval battles.

Moderna Museet
(p58)

With its world-class collection housed in a fabulous building, Moderna is a must-see for art fans. It also has a stellar bookshop, an acclaimed restaurant and consistently well-executed temporary exhibits.

Fotografiska (p70)

An impressive and stylish hall of photography, Fotografiska never fails to present thorough, high-calibre exhibitions, usually several at a time. The location is cool, and there's a top-notch cafe-bar.

Stadshuset (p100)

This imposing building defines the Stockholm skyline, with its blocky silhouette and waterside perch. Inside is the glittering Golden Hall, frescoes by Prins Eugen and the inspiring Nobel Prize banquet room.

Stockholm
Local Life

Insider tips to help you find the real cit

Once you've checked off the must-see sights on your list, it's time to find out what Stockholm is like for locals. Be warned: there will be shopping.

Norrmalm Shopping (p38)

▸ High-fashion boutiques
▸ Beautiful architecture

Whether you're after traditional handmade Swedish crafts, fine crystal, outdoors equipment or the most exclusive high-fashion brands, you'll find it in Norrmalm's glittering shops.

Escaping to Djurgården (p60)

▸ Quiet paths
▸ Green spaces

Though it's only a short stroll across a bridge from the heart of the city, Djurgården feels like a quiet, green oasis. The parklike island is mostly undeveloped woodlands, laced with fields and trails where fitness-savvy locals go to run or just relax.

Södermalm Bar-Hopping (p72)

▸ Bars full of character
▸ Characters in the bars

Hard to beat for atmosphere and people-watching alike, Södermalm is known as the arty-funky neighbourhood for good reason. Ranging from ultra-chic cocktail bars to antique Swedish beer halls to basement dives, the bars and pubs here reward intrepid exploration.

Opulent Östermalm (p86)

▸ Culinary delights
▸ Elegant buildings and boulevards

Live large in this up-market yet non-stodgy neighbourhood: do some window-shopping, splash out on a decadent meal or a fancy cocktail, pick up some designer fashio or just wander down a street lined with gorgeou old buildings and feel lik a million bucks.

Museums of Gärdet & Ladugårdsgärdet (p94)

▸ Excellent museums
▸ Parklike setting

Some of the best museums in Stockholm, especially for families, ar located in this beautiful, tree-lined neighbourhoo where you can also find stunning city views.

Djurgården (p60)

Shopping in Norrmalm (p38)

Other great places to experience the city like a local:

Stompin' at Stampen (p34)

Lisa Larsson Second Hand (p81)

Special Tea (p91)

Classy Cocktails (p92)

Vintage Books (p93)

Street Eats (p105)

Urban Beaches (p107)

Park Life (p116)

Classic Cafe (p119)

Stockholm
Day Planner

Day One

Get an early start your first day to beat the crowds to Gamla Stan. Fortify yourself with a coffee and pastry, then line up for a tour of the royal palace, **Kungliga Slottet** (p24). The palace tour includes three other museums – the Museum Tre Kronor, devoted to Stockholm's original castle; the Royal Treasury; and Gustav III's Antikmuseum – all worth a look. Allow two or three hours to see everything.

After that, you'll need lunch: head for the veggie buffet at **Hermitage** (p33). Walk off lunch with a leisurely stroll from Gamla Stan across Norrbro and along the water's edge until you reach the footbridge, called Skeppsholmsbron, that will take you across to the island of Skeppsholmen. Here you can visit the contemporary-art powerhouse that is **Moderna Museet** (p58), then stop in for something completely different – a collection of East Asian antiquities – at the **Östasiatiska Museet** (p66).

Afterward, walk back over the footbridge, to Norrmalm and back along the waterfront to settle in for a drink at the bar of the **Grand Hôtel Stockholm** (p147). For dinner, make your way to a counter seat at the Opera's **Bakfickan** (p44) for a decadent meal of Swedish classic cuisine.

Day Two

On your second day, it's time to check a couple of Djurgården favourites off the list. First, spend a few hours exploring **Skansen** (p52), the open-air museum that calls itself 'Sweden in miniature'. Be sure to see the animals the Nordic zoo, and don't miss the glass-blowers' cottage. You could spend the day here, but there's more to see!

Stop for lunch in the outdoor courtyard at the **Blå Porten Café** (p66), near the Skansen gates. Then head to nearby **Vasamuseet** (p56), a purpose-built museum dedicated to the resuscitation of a sunken battleship. The multimedia displays here should keep you occupied for at least an hour or two. If you have time afterward, pop next door to the **Spritmuseum** (p63) to get the low-down on the complicated history and social significance of booze in Sweden.

Take the ferry from Djurgården across to Norrmalm – summer only, but it's an easy walk – and make your way toward Stureplan. Have an elegant dinner at the seafood-savvy **Sturehof** (p91), and drinks in its tiny, exclusive bar, before exploring the surrounding clubs, including **Sturecompagniet** (p92), **Spy Bar** (p92) and **Laroy** (p92).

ort on time?
e've arranged Stockholm's must-sees into these day-by-day itineraries to make
re you see the very best of the city in the time you have available.

ay Three

Three days in Stockholm will give you enough time to see a few of e further-flung highlights in the area. art with a visit to **Drottningholm** .09), the royal family's summer palace. worth taking the one-hour guided ur – the earliest one starts when doors en at 10am, which allows you time get here. Fortify yourself with coffee d cakes afterward at **Drottningholms viljongen** (p109).

Back in town, hop aboard a ferry to Vaxholm, the gateway to the ockholm archipelago. Start with lunch **Waxholms Hotell** (p121), preferably ts covered outdoor terrace bar – and Baltic herring appears on the menu any form, your choice is clear. Then end the rest of the afternoon wander- ; the crooked, hilly streets of the pretty age and browsing in shops, perhaps pping for a pastry at **Vaxholms Bak-** (p121), until it's time for your return at to Stockholm.

Back in the city, head over to **Berns Salonger** (p45) for a light ner and a nightcap. If you're up to inger here for music and dancing in ighly designed and historically rich vironment.

Day Four

On day four, start with a tour of **Stadshuset** (p100), the surpris- ingly pretty City Hall. Then hop the tunnelbana to Östermalm to catch up on some Viking lore at **Historiska Museet** (p84), where displays include everything from skulls and armour to ancient coins and elaborate gold-filigree necklaces.

Queue up for lunch at **Lisa Elmqvist** (p90) inside the fabu- lous Östermalms Saluhall, where you can browse for specialty foods to take home as gifts. While you're in shopping mode stop in at handicraft specialist **Svensk Slöjd** (p93) for authentic and expertly crafted souvenirs.

Take a tunnelbana to Medbor- garplatsen to explore the funky southern part of town, Södermalm, with its shops and galleries and hipster hangouts. Walk up Götgatan toward the Slussen area, but hang a hard right up the hill just before you reach it – this places you upon the Söder cliffs at dusk, where you'll enjoy an unparalleled view of the city. From here, take the stairs down to visit absorbing **Fotografiska** (p70) gallery – then it's back up the hill for a well-earned buffet dinner at **Hermans Trädgårdscafé** (p76).

Need to Know

For more information,
see Survival Guide (p145)

Currency
Krona (Skr)

Language
Swedish

Visas
Citizens of EU countries can enter Sweden with a passport. Visitors from Australia, New Zealand, Canada and the US can stay in Sweden without a visa for up to 90 days. Some nationalities need a Schengen visa in advance, good for 90 days.

Money
ATMs are widely available, and credit cards are almost universally accepted.

Mobile Phones
Most mobile phones work in Sweden, though often with hefty roaming fees. Local SIM cards also work in most phones, with the benefit of a local number and no roaming charges; ask your provider to unlock your phone for international travel.

Time
Central European Time (GMT/UTC plus 1 hour)

Plugs & Adaptors
Plugs have two round pins; electrical current is 220V. North American visitors will require an adaptor and a transformer.

Tipping
Service is figured into the bill, but with an evening meal a 10% to 15% tip is customary.

① Before You Go

Your Daily Budget

Budget less than Skr1000
► Dorm bed or camping site Skr200–30◯
► Fast-food lunch or sandwich Skr55–85
► 24-hour bus and metro ticket Skr115
► Museum admission Skr100

Midrange Skr1000–2000
► Double room Skr800–1600
► Restaurant meal Skr100–200
► Happy-hour beer or wine Skr35–95

Top end more than Skr2000
► Double room Skr1600–2600
► Upscale dinner and drinks Skr350–600
► Taxi from airport Skr520

Useful Websites

Visit Stockholm (www.visitstockholm.com)
Official tourist-bureau website, great for planning and inspiration.

Swedish Institute (www.si.se) Well-informe◯
perspectives on all aspects of Swedish culture.

Lonely Planet (www.lonelyplanet.com/stockholm) Planning and inspiration.

Advance Planning

Three months before Book a top-end ho◯◯ or sought-after B&B; secure tickets to popular shows or music festivals.

One month before Reserve a table at a f◯ restaurant; buy your Stockholm discoun◯ cards; plan day trips.

One week before Double-check museu◯ closing times and days.

2 Arriving in Stockholm

ockholm Arlanda Airport (www.swedavia. , the main airport serving Stockholm, is ut 45km north of city centre, well con- cted by bus and express train.

andful of domestic flights arrive at **mma Airport**, only 8km west of the city tre and on the tunnelbana line. **Skavsta port** (www.skavsta.se), 100km south of ckholm, is mostly served by budget riers like Ryanair.

From Stockholm anda Airport

estination	Best Transport
ty Centre	Arlanda Express train or Flygbuss
eater ockholm	Tunnelbana from city centre or taxi

At the Airport

anda Airport The international arrival has ATMs, currency exchange windows, venience stores, restrooms, automatic f-service ticket machines for various trans- t options into the city centre, and a coffee p. The main hall of the airport, called Sky- y, has all the usual services: information sks, shops and restaurants, an adjoining el, newsstands, internet-ready computer minals, more ticket machines, and luggage rage. All terminals have access to the anda Express train to the centre. Car-hire nters are in a separate building; a free ttle bus connects them to the airport.

3 Getting Around

Public transport in Stockholm is extremely efficient and reliable, though not particularly cheap. It's run by **Storstockholms Loka- ltrafik** (SL; ☎08-600 10 00; www.sl.se; Centralstationen, Sergels Torg; single trip Skr25-50, unlimited 24hr/72hr/7-day pass Skr115/230/300), which has information desks at Centralstationen and at several tunnelbana stations. Nearly always, passes good for longer periods are better value than tickets for single trips. Students and seniors pay half price. All types of tickets or passes can be bought at tunnelbana stations and Pressbyrå newsstands. There's a good trip planner at http://reseplanerare.resrobot.se.

Ⓜ Tunnelbana (Metro)

The tunnelbana is the city's underground rail line, and the most useful mode of transport for most of Stockholm. It's well run, clean and easy to navigate.

🚌 Bus

The city bus system, using the same tickets or passes as the tunnelbana, is ideal for reaching places between tunnelbana stops, as well as some attractions in the suburbs. You must have your ticket or pass before boarding.

🚗 Taxi

There are several reliable taxi companies in Stockholm, all with fairly similar rates.

🚲 Cycling

Stockholm is a great city for cycling, with well-marked bike lanes, dedicated cycling paths in most neighbourhoods, and around 90 self-service bicycle-hire stands across the city.

Stockholm
Neighbourhoods

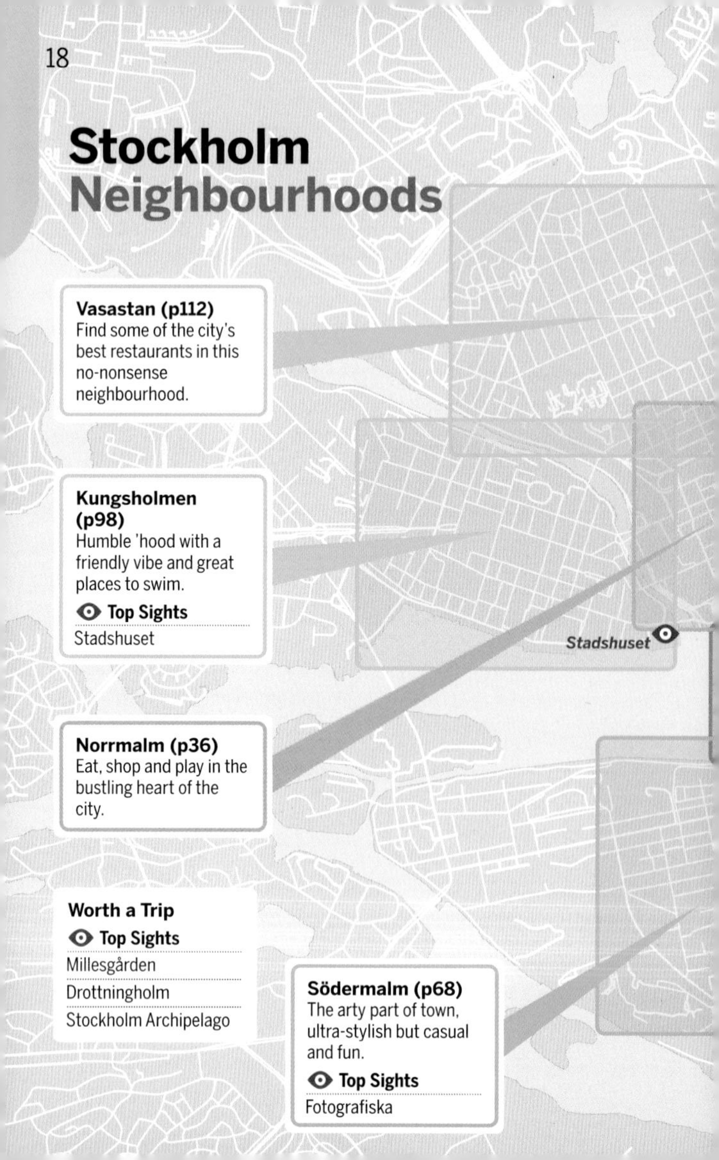

Vasastan (p112)
Find some of the city's best restaurants in this no-nonsense neighbourhood.

Kungsholmen (p98)
Humble 'hood with a friendly vibe and great places to swim.
⊙ Top Sights
Stadshuset

Stadshuset ⊙

Norrmalm (p36)
Eat, shop and play in the bustling heart of the city.

Worth a Trip
⊙ Top Sights
Millesgården
Drottningholm
Stockholm Archipelago

Södermalm (p68)
The arty part of town, ultra-stylish but casual and fun.
⊙ Top Sights
Fotografiska

Östermalm (p82)
Dress up and scope out the beautiful people over a flute of bubbly.

◉ Top Sights

Historiska Museet

Djurgården & Skeppsholmen (p50)
A parklike oasis with most of the city's best museums.

◉ Top Sights

Skansen

Vasamuseet

Moderna Museet

◉ *Historiska Museet*

◉ *Vasamuseet*

◉ *Skansen*

◉ *Kungliga Slottet*

◉ *Moderna Museet*

◉ *Fotografiska*

Gamla Stan (p22)
A medieval labyrinth of cobblestone streets and saffron-hued buildings.

◉ Top Sights

Kungliga Slottet

Explore
Stockholm

Worth a Trip

Streetside dining, Österlånggatan, Gamla Stan
JORG GREUEL / GETTY IMAGES ©

Explore

Gamla Stan

The old town, Gamla Stan, is one of Europe's most arresting historic hubs, all story-book buildings, imposing palaces and razor-thin cobblestone streets.

The Sights in a Day

☀ Fuel up with a decadent pastry and coffee at **Grillska Husets Konditori** (p34), then hop over to **Kungliga Slottet** (p24), the royal palace, to get in with an early tour group. After the tour, make sure to peek into the Museum Tre Kronor in the basement, as well as the Royal Treasury and Gustav III's Antikmuseum. If you finish up around noon you'll catch the impressive Changing of the Guard, with its fanfare and marching band.

☀ Wander down to Stora Nygatan for a healthy buffet lunch at **Hermitage** (p33), then stroll along toward Riddarholmen to admire the lovely iron-spired **Riddarholmskyrkan** (p31) and its surrounding islet. Crossing back over to Gamla Stan, take a look inside **Storkyrkan** (p30), then settle in for some inspiration and innovation at the **Nobelmuseet** (p30).

🌙 After all that museum-going, you'll want to sit for a moment with a latte or hot cocoa and do some hardcore people-watching from the terrace of **Chokladkoppen** (p34). Then wander some shopping streets or go for a happy-hour cocktail at **Le Rouge** (p35) before grabbing dinner at the ultra-traditional **Den Gyldene Freden** (p34).

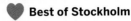

👁 **Top Sights**

Kungliga Slottet (p24)

💜 **Best of Stockholm**

Eating

Kryp In (p33)

Hermitage (p33)

Den Gyldene Freden (p34)

Drinking

Monks Porter House (p35)

Le Rouge (p35)

Museums & Galleries

Kungliga Slottet (p24)

Nobelmuseet (p30)

Medeltidsmuseet (p30)

Getting There

Ⓜ **Tunnelbana** Gamla Stan, Slussen

🚌 **Bus** 43, 46, 55, 59 to Slottsbacken

Walk The old town is an easy stroll from the city centre.

Top Sights
Kungliga Slottet

The imposing, boxy royal palace, Kungliga Slottet, dominates tiny Gamla Stan and is well worth a visit. It was built on the ruins of Tre Kronor castle, most of which burned to the ground in 1697. The north wing survived and was incorporated into the new building. Designed by the court architect Nicodemus Tessin the Younger, it took 57 years to complete. With 608 rooms, it's the world's largest royal castle still used for its original purpose. (The royal family has lived here since 1754.)

👁 Map p18, E2

www.kungahuset.se

adult/child Skr150/75

🕐 10am–5pm mid-May–mid-Sep, closed Mon rest of year

🚍 43, 46, 55, 59 Slottsbacken, Ⓜ Gamla Stan

Don't Miss

Changing of the Guard
It's worth timing your visit to see the Changing of the Guard, which takes place in the outer courtyard at 12.15pm Monday to Saturday and 1.15pm on Sundays and public holidays May through August, but only on Wednesday, Saturday, Sunday and public holidays September to May.

Museum Tre Kronor
This museum displays the foundations of 13th-century defensive walls and items rescued from the castle during the 1697 fire. It describes how the fire started (a watchman was off flirting with a kitchen maid) and vividly explains the meaning of 'run the gauntlet' (which in 1697 was the punishment for flirting with kitchen maids while fire destroyed the castle).

Gustav III's State Bedchamber
King Gustav III, whose efforts to reconsolidate power for the throne in the early part of his reign made him unpopular with the nobility, died here in 1792 – a full 13 days after an assassin shot him during a masquerade ball. He survived just long enough to keep up appearances and suppress the attempted coup.

Silver Throne
Queen Kristina's silver throne, in the Hall of State, was rescued from the Tre Kronor fire. It was a gift to the queen from Swedish statesman Magnus Gabriel de la Gardie (son of Ebba Brahe, who had an affair with King Gustavus Adolphus). The impressive hall was designed by architects Nicodemus Tessin the Younger and Carl Hårleman.

☑ Top Tips

▶ Beat the crowds: for the best experience, arrive when the palace opens at 10am.

▶ Free 45-minute tours in English start at 11am and 2pm mid-May to mid-September, and at 2pm and 3pm the rest of the year – they're well worth taking.

▶ Admission to the palace also includes the nearby Museum Tre Kronor, the Royal Treasury and the Antikmuseum.

▶ Tickets are valid for seven days.

▶ The apartments are occasionally closed for royal business; closures are noted on the website.

✗ Take a Break

In summer, there's a small cafe (open from 6 June through to late August) with outdoor tables in the castle's inner courtyard, serving light lunches, coffee and pastries. Kungliga Slottet is also a cobblestone's throw from the cosy Chokladkoppen (p34).

Understand
Changing Fashions

Tour guides at Kungliga Slottet emphasise that the palace is not a museum, with rooms preserved in amber, but rather a working government building. (The king and queen still have their main offices here, and the palace is where they meet with visiting dignitaries and hold special events – this also means occasional closures of all or part of the building may occur.) Though the palace contains fine examples of baroque and rococo furnishings and interiors, and a few corners here and there are extremely well preserved, each room also bears the fingerprints of the many generations who have lived here.

Karl XI Gallery
One of the prettiest rooms in the palace, and still used today for royal functions, the decadent Karl XI Gallery was inspired by Versailles' Hall of Mirrors and is considered the finest example of Swedish late baroque.

Royal Treasury
The Royal Treasury (Skattkammaren) contains ceremonial crowns, sceptres and other regalia of the Swedish monarchy, including Lovisa Ulrika's crown, a 1696 baptismal font (still used today for royal baptisms), tapestries rescued from the 1697 fire and a 16th-century sword that belonged to Gustav Vasa.

Antikmuseum
Gustav III's Museum of Antiquities (summer only) displays sculpture mostly collected by King Gustav III during his Italian journeys (the requisite 'grand tour') during the 1780s. For most of the Swedish public, this was a first glimpse of classical sculpture. The galleries were renovated starting in the 1950s in order to keep the collection safely in its original home.

Royal Chapel
A chapel has stood in the royal palace since the 1200s, but this version of it – dating from the palace reopening in 1754 – was a 50-year project, overseen by Nicodemus Tessin the Younger. (In the early days, though, the royal family took mass in their own private chambers.)

Kungliga Slottet

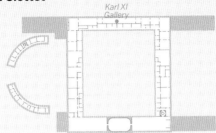

Karl XI
Gallery

First Floor

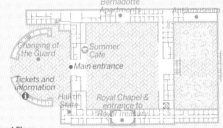

Bernadotte
Apartments

Antikmuseum

Changing of
the Guard

Summer
Cafe

• Main entrance

Tickets and
information

Hall of
State

Royal Chapel &
entrance to
Royal Treasury

Ground Floor

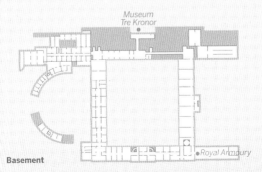

Museum
Tre Kronor

• Royal Armoury

Basement

A **B** **C** **D**

1

Riksbron

Strömparte

Helgeandsho

Centralbron

Vasabron

Riksdagshuset

⦿ 8

Norra
Järnvägsbron

Riksgatan

Strömsborg

Bankkajen Stallb

2

Rådhusgränd

Mynttor

Norra
Riddarholmshamnen

Riddarhuskajen

Riddarhusgränd

Myntgatan

Arkivgatan

RIDDARHOLMEN

Riddarhustorget

Storkyrkobrinke

3

Evert
Taubes
Terrass

Birger
Jarls Torg

⟟ 10

Wrangelska Backen

15
⦿

Stora Nygatan

7 ⦿

Lilla Nygatan

Riddarholmskyrkan

Munkbrogatan

5 ⦿ Postmuseum

Södra Riddarholmshamnen

Munkbroleden

Schönfelts Grän

4

Södra Järnvägsbron

M Gamla
Stan

Tyska
Brinke

Riddarfjärden

Mälartorget

5

Södra
Järnvägsbron

Centralbron

Ⓝ 0 ——————————— 200 m
0 ——————————— 0.1 miles

E Strömbron
Medeltidsmuseet
Norrbro
Slottskajen
Norrström
National-museum

F
G
H

Skeppsholmsbron

Kungliga Slottet
ttre gården
Royal Armoury
2
Skeppsbrokajen

Slottsbacken

Kungliga Myntkabinettet 6
Telegrafgränd

Storkyrkan

elmuseet
1 Trädgårdsgatan
14
Bredgränd
Kråkgränd
16 Nygränd
Brunnsgränd
Skottgränd
Drakens Gränd

Stortorget
Köpmangatan
13 Gamla Stan
19

Skomakargatan
Västerlånggatan
18
Prästgatan
Svartmangatan
Kindstugatan
Själagårdsgatan
Baggensgatan

Tyska Skolgränd

Johannesgränd
Packhusgränd
11
Tullgränd
Skeppsbron

stedts
ränd
Kornhamnstorg
Järntorget
Norra Bankogränd

Munkbroleden

Slussplan

Strömmen

Norrström

For reviews see	
⊙ Top Sights	p24
⊙ Sights	p30
✕ Eating	p33
⊖ Drinking	p34
⊖ Shopping	p35

Sights

Nobelmuseet
MUSEUM

1 📍 Map p28, E3

Nobelmuseet presents the history of the Nobel Prizes and their recipients, with a focus on the intellectual and cultural aspects of invention. It's a slick space with fascinating displays, including short films on the theme of creativity, interviews with laureates like Ernest Hemingway and Martin Luther King, and cafe chairs signed by the visiting prize recipients. The free guided tours are recommended (in English at 10.15am, 11.15am, 1pm, 3pm, 4pm and 6pm in summer). (www.nobelmuseet.se; Stortorget; adult/child Skr100/70; ⏰10am-8pm; 🄼Gamla Stan)

Royal Armoury
MUSEUM

2 📍 Map p28, F2

The Royal Armoury is housed in the cellar vaults of the palace but has a separate admission fee. It's a family attic of sorts, crammed with engrossing memorabilia spanning more than 500 years of royal childhoods, coronations, weddings and murders. Meet Gustav II Adolf's stuffed battle steed, Streiff; see the costume Gustav III wore to the masquerade ball on the night he was shot, in 1792; or let the kids try on a suit of armour in the playroom. (Livrustkammaren; 📞08-402 30 30; www.livrustkammaren.se; Slottsbacken 3; adult/child Skr90/free; ⏰10am-5pm; 🚌43, 46, 55, 59 Slottsbacken, 🄼Gamla Stan)

Storkyrkan
CHURCH

3 📍 Map p28, E2

The one-time venue for royal weddings and coronations, Storkyrkan is both Stockholm's oldest building (consecrated in 1306) and its cathedral. Behind a baroque facade, the Gothic-baroque interior includes extravagant royal-box pews designed by Nicodemus Tessin the Younger, as well as German Berndt Notke's dramatic sculpture *St George and the Dragon*, commissioned by Sten Sture the Elder to commemorate his victory over the Danes in 1471. (Great Church; www.stockholmsdomkyrkoforsamling.se; Trångsund 1; adult/child Skr40/free; ⏰9am-4pm; 🄼Gamla Stan)

Medeltidsmuseet
MUSEUM

4 📍 Map p28, E1

Tucked beneath the bridge that links Gamla Stan and Norrmalm, this child-friendly museum was established when construction workers preparing to build a car park here in the late 1970s unearthed foundations from the 1530s. The ancient walls were preserved as found, and a museum was built around them. The circular plan leads visitors through faithful reconstructions of typical homes, markets and workshops from medieval Stockholm. Tickets are valid for one year and will also get you into Stockholms Stadsmuseum (p76). (Medieval Museum; www.medeltidsmuseet.stockholm.se; Strömparterren; adult/child Skr100/free; ⏰noon-5pm Tue-Sun, to 7pm Wed; 🚼; 🚌62, 65, Gustav Adolfs torg)

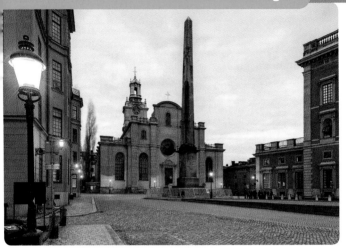

Storkyrkan

Postmuseum
MUSEUM

5 Map p28, D4

Examining almost four centuries of
Swedish postal history, the Postmuseum is not as mind-numbing as it
sounds. It's actually rather evocative,
featuring old mail carriages, kitsch
postcards and a cute children's post
office for budding postal workers.
(☑08-781 17 59; www.postmuseum.posten.
se; Lilla Nygatan 6; adult/child Skr60/free;
☺11am-4pm Wed-Sun; ⓜGamla Stan)

Kungliga Myntkabinettet
MUSEUM

6 Map p28, F2

Across the plaza from the royal palace,
Kungliga Myntkabinettet gleams with
a priceless collection of currency spanning 2600 years. Treasures include Viking silver and the world's oldest coin
(from 625 BC), largest coin (a Swedish
copper plate weighing 19.7kg) and first
banknote (issued in Sweden in 1661).
(Royal Coin Cabinet; ☑08-519 553 04; www.
myntkabinettet.se; Slottsbacken 6; adult/
child Skr70/free, Mon free; ☺11am-5pm;
ⓜGamla Stan)

Riddarholmskyrkan
CHURCH

7 Map p28, B3

The strikingly beautiful Riddarholmskyrkan, on the equally pretty and
under-visited islet of Riddarholmen,
was built by Franciscan monks in
the late 13th century. It has been the
royal necropolis since the burial of

Government & Politics

The current king of Sweden, Karl XVI Gustaf, is the seventh of the Bernadotte dynasty. He became crown prince at age four and king at 27 (in 1973). He met Queen Silvia, a German-Brazilian who was neither a royal nor a member of the nobility, at the Munich Olympic Games. Their eldest daughter, Crown Princess Victoria, will be the next monarch. (Since 1980 it has been Swedish policy that the first-born is heir to the throne regardless of gender.)

The king is head of state and an important figure, but apolitical, with mostly ceremonial and ambassadorial duties. Sweden is governed by Parliament, with elections every four years.

Despite the country's middle-way steadiness over the long term, recent changes in the economy and the political mood have led some to question their assumptions. For decades Sweden was viewed by left-leaning outsiders as an almost utopian model of a socialist state, a successful experiment that gave hope to progressives everywhere. This is still more or less true. But as the country has grown, it has had to adjust to modern realities – both economic and sociopolitical – and some cracks have begun to appear in the facade.

The Social Democrats, who held a majority of the government (and therefore shaped national policy, most notably the famous 'cradle to grave' welfare state) for most of the past 85 years, have seen their influence wane in recent years.

The 2010 election saw the Social Democrats' worst results since 1921: they won just over 30% of the seats in Parliament. The Alliance Party won a second term (173 of the 349 seats), but unemployment was high and by 2012 the Social Democrats had regained some favour. By the September 2014 election, the Social Democrats were back: Alliance Party leader Fredrik Reinfeldt lost his bid for a third term, and Social Democrats leader Stefan Löfven became prime minister. The biggest factor in the election was the right-wing nationalist Sweden Democrats party, which saw twice the support it had previously – going from 20 to 49 seats, making it the third-largest party in Parliament. This promises to create friction, as the other parties have said they won't cooperate with the Sweden Democrats.

Magnus Ladulås in 1290, and is home to the armorial glory of the Seraphim knightly order. There's a guided tour in English at noon (included with admission) and occasional concerts. Holiday closures are frequent; check the website for updates. Admission fee is by credit card only. (Riddarholmen Church; ☎08-402 61 30; www.kungahuset. se; Riddarholmen; adult/child Skr50/free; ⏱10am-5pm mid-May–mid-Sep; 🚌3, 53 Riddarhustorget, Ⓜ Gamla Stan)

Riksdagshuset
BUILDING

8 ◉ Map p28, D1

Technically situated on Helgeands-holmen, the little island in the middle of Norrström, rather than on Gamla Stan, the Swedish Parliament building is an unexpected pleasure to visit. The building consists of two parts: the older front section (facing downstream) dates from the early 20th century, but the other more modern part contains the current debating chamber. (Swedish Parliament; ☎08-786 48 62; www.riksdagen. se; Riksgatan 3; admission free; ⏱1hr tours in English noon, 1pm, 2pm & 3pm Mon-Fri mid-Jun–Aug, 1.30pm Sat & Sun Oct–mid-Jun)

Eating

Kryp In
SWEDISH $$$

9 ❌ Map p28, E3

Small but perfectly formed, this spot wows diners with creative takes on traditional Swedish dishes. Expect the likes of salmon carpaccio or smoked

reindeer salad followed by a gorgeous, spirit-warming saffron aioli shellfish stew. The service is seamless and the atmosphere classy without being stuffy. The brief weekend lunch menu (Skr119 to Skr158) is a bargain. Book ahead. (☎08-20 88 41; www.restaurang-krypin.nu; Prästgatan 17; starters Skr135-195, mains Skr195-285; ⏱5-11pm Mon-Fri, 12.30-4pm & 5-11pm Sat & Sun; Ⓜ Gamla Stan)

Hermitage
VEGETARIAN $$

10 ❌ Map p28, D3

Herbivores love Hermitage for its simple, tasty, vegetarian buffet, easily one of the best restaurant bargains in Gamla Stan. Salad, homemade bread, tea and coffee are included in the price. (Stora Nygatan 11; lunch/dinner & weekends Skr110/120; ⏱11am-8pm Mon-Sat, noon-4pm Sun; 🌿; Ⓜ Gamla Stan)

Den Gyldene Freden SWEDISH $$$

11 Map p28, F4

Open since 1722, this venerable barrel-vaulted restaurant run by the Swedish Academy, is where (rumour has it) its members meet to decide the winners of the Nobel Prize. Personally, we think it should go to the chefs, whose sublime offerings include civilised *husmanskost* dishes like roast lamb with chanterelles, cabbage and country cheese, or old-school Swedish meatballs. (☑08-24 97 60; www.gyldenefreden.se; Österlånggatan 51; lunch Skr165-265, dinner mains Skr180-370; ☉lunch Mon-Fri, dinner Mon-Sat; Ⓜ Gamla Stan)

Chokladkoppen CAFE $

12 Map p28, E3

Arguably Stockholm's best-loved cafe, hole-in-the-wall Chokladkoppen sits slap bang on the old town's enchanting main square. It's a gay-friendly

spot, with cute waiters, a look-at-me summer terrace and yummy grub like broccoli-and-blue-cheese pie and scrumptious cakes. (www.chokladkoppen.se; Stortorget 18; cakes Skr40-80; ☉9am-11pm summer, shorter hours rest of year; Ⓜ Gamla Stan)

Grillska Husets Konditori BAKERY, CAFE $

13 Map p28, E3

The cafe and bakery run by Stockholms Stadsmission, the chain of secondhand charity shops, is a top-notch spot for a sweet treat or a sandwich, especially when warm weather allows for seating at the outdoor tables in Gamla Stan's main square. There's a bakery shop attached, selling goodies and rustic breads to take away. (☑08-68 42 33 64; www.stadsmissionen.se; Stortorget 3; sandwiches Skr25-75; ☉9am-6pm Mon-Fri, 10am-6pm Sat & Sun; Ⓜ Gamla Stan)

Hairy Pig Deli DELI $

14 Map p28, F3

Follow your nose to this cute little corner deli, where the personable owners make all their own sausages and serve beer brewed by a family friend. Try the sausage of the day (Skr65), a salami and cheese baguette (Skr85), a charcuterie plate, an assortment of tapas or the excellent salad with house-made salami and cheese from the Stockholm archipelago. (Håriga Grisen; ☑073-800 26 23; www.hairypigdeli.se; Österlånggatan 9; mains Skr65-100, tapas Skr45-55; ☉5-9pm Tue-Fri, noon-10pm Sat; Ⓜ Gamla Stan)

Drinking

Monks Porter House PUB

15 Map p28, C3

This cavernous brewpub has an epic beer list, including 56 taps, many of which are made here or at the Monks microbrewery in Vasastan. Everything we tried was delicious, especially the Monks Orange Ale – your best bet is to ask the bartender for a recommendation (or a taste). Check online for beer-tasting events. (☎08-23 12 12; www.monkscafe.se; Munkbron 11; ☉from 6pm Tue-Sat; Ⓜ Gamla Stan)

Le Rouge BAR

16 Map p28, F3

Fin-de-siècle Paris is the inspiration for this decadent lounge in Gamla Stan, a melange of rich red velvet, tasselled lampshades, inspired cocktails and French bistro grub. (The adjoining restaurant is run by two of Stockholm's hottest chefs, Danyel Couet and Melker Andersson.) DJs hit the decks Thursday to Saturday. (☎08-50 52 44 30; Österlånggatan 17; ☉11.30am-2pm & 5pm-1am Mon-Fri, 5pm-1am Sat)

Torget BAR

17 Map p28, D4

For camp and Campari, it's hard to beat this sparkling gay bar – think rotating chandeliers, mock-baroque touches and different themed evenings, from live burlesque to handbag-swinging *schlager*. The crowd is a good source of info on upcoming underground parties, so grab yourself a champers and chat away. (www.torgetbaren.com; Mälartorget 13; ☉5pm-midnight, to 1am Sun; Ⓜ Gamla Stan)

Shopping

Science Fiction Bookshop BOOKS

18 Map p28, E4

In some ways this seems an unlikely location for a science fiction–fantasy comic bookshop, but in other ways it makes perfect sense. Regardless, this is the place to come for comics and graphic novels both mainstream and esoteric (in English and Swedish), as well as books, games, toys and posters. Friendly staff will help you find obscure treasures. (www.sfbok.se; Västerlånggatan 48; ☉10am-7pm Mon-Fri, to 5pm Sat, noon-5pm Sun; Ⓜ Gamla Stan)

Studio Lena M GIFTS

19 Map p28, E3

This tiny, dimly lit shop is crammed with adorable prints and products featuring the graphic design work of Lena M, as well as other like-minded artists. It's a great place to find a unique – and uniquely Swedish – gift to bring home, or even just a cute postcard. (www.lenamdesign.se; Kindstugan 14; Ⓜ Gamla Stan)

Explore

Norrmalm

The modern heart of the city, Norrmalm is where most visits to Stockholm begin: it's home to the main train and bus stations, Centralstationen and Cityterminalen respectively. It's also where you'll find the highest concentration of schmancy retail boutiques, glamorous bars and restaurants, fabulous hotels and noteworthy cultural institutions.

The Sights in a Day

☀ Start your day with a dose of fine art, courtesy of the National Museum – it's undergoing repairs until 2017, but exhibits from its collection are being shown at the very pretty **Konstakademien** (p42), whose Tessin-designed building holds several galleries as well as its classrooms. Afterward, get ready for some serious interior-decorating voyeurism with a tour of the **Hallwylska Museet** (p42), the former home of a wealthy count and countess who collected objets d'art with the intent of eventually displaying them to the public.

☀ Continue the decorative theme but in a slightly different form with a visit to the **Dansmuseet** (p42), where you'll see hundreds of dance costumes and props from around the world. Fuel up at the attached bistro-cafe before moving on.

☾ Wrap up the afternoon at the **Medelhavsmuseet** (p42), filled with fascinating artefacts and artwork from the Medieval world, notably Egyptian lore and ancient Greek and Roman sculpture. There's also a great cafe here, if you're still hungry.

For a local's day in Norrmalm, see p38.

○ Local Life

♥ Best of Stockholm

Eating

Nightlife

Music

Getting There

Ⓜ **Tunnelbana** T-Centralen, Kungsträdgården

🚌 **Bus** Cityterminalen, Norrmalmstorg, Sergels Torg

🚊 **Tram** 7

Local Life
Norrmalm Shopping

Ever wonder how Stockholmers manage to look so fashionable all the time? Shopping is a sport here, and Norrmalm is one of the best places to do it well. Its chic storefronts peddle everything from traditional handmade crafts to fine crystal, outdoors equipment to the most exclusive high-fashion brands. And a good stretch of the district is pedestrian-only, so you can focus on the task at hand.

❶ Norrmalmstorg
Start your mission at the heart of the district, the wide-open square of Norrmalmstorg. At its easternmost edge you'll find the epitome of Stockholm cool, **Acne Studios** (☎08-611 64 11; www.acnestudios.com; Norrmalmstorg 2; ⏱10am-7pm Mon-Fri, to 5pm Sat, noon-4pm Sun; ⓜÖstermalmstorg), with a shop that closely resembles a fashion museum. In the same block you'll find the impossible-to-resist **Marimekko**

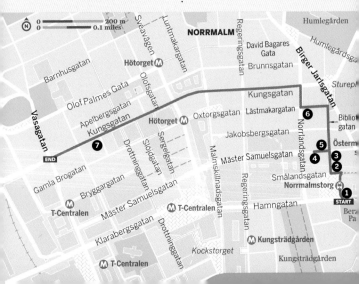

(☏08-440 32 75; www.marimekko.com; Norrmalmstorg 4; ⏰10am-6.30pm Mon-Fri, to 5pm Sat; Ⓜ Östermalmstorg), purveyors of ultra-fun patterned textiles.

❷ Biblioteksgatan

At the north end of Norrmalmstorg is this pedestrianised shopping street, lined wall-to-wall with hot brand names. Right on the corner is an outlet of the groundbreaking Swedish fashion designer **Filippa K** (www.filippa-k.com; Biblioteksgatan 2).

❸ Mäster Samuelsgatan

This street, which crosses Biblioteksgatan, is home to a dense population of big-name fashion. Off to the right is **Whyred** (☏08-660 01 70; www.whyred.se; Mäster Samuelsgatan 5; ⏰10am-7pm Mon-Fri, to 5pm Sat, noon-4pm Sun; Ⓜ Östermalmstorg), beloved for men's sweaters and women's shoes, among other things; next to that is the relatively new **BLK DNM** (www.blkdnm.com; Mäster Samuelsgatan 1), with its painfully hip jackets and other clothing by designer Johan Lindeberg. Across the street is **Fifth Avenue Shoe Repair** (Mäster Samuelsgatan 2), another cutting-edge design crew.

❹ Cow Parfymeri

A great place to pick up gifts to bring home, **Cow Parfymeri** (☏08-611 15 04; www.cowparfymeri.se; Mäster Samuelsgatan 9; ⏰11am-6pm Mon-Fri, to 4pm Sat; Ⓜ Östermalmstorg) is a cool cosmetics temple with a trendsetting range of perfumes, sticks and shades. Pick up rock-chic cosmetics from Urban Decay and Vincent Longo, or spray yourself silly with hard-to-find fragrances from Paris and New York.

❺ Urban Outfitters

Worth a stop for its exterior as much as for its hipster-bait wares, **Urban Outfitters** (Biblioteksgatan 5) is in a building that used to house the Röda Kvarn (Moulin Rouge), a gorgeous vintage picture palace. While the projectors have gone, the heritage features remain, from decadent chandeliers to beautiful hardwood details. Fitting rooms line the grand old stage behind a kitschy mock-chateau facade, and the upstairs foyers now premiere the work of new Stockholm artists.

❻ Espresso Stop

By now you're probably ready for a break. The lovely **Bianchi Cafe & Cycles** (www.bianchicafecycles.com; Norrlandsgatan 20) is an ideal spot for an espresso and a pastry.

❼ Kungsgatan

You'll pass by all manner of retail outlets here, both local and global, including the fun outdoor market and food hall at Hötorget. Several blocks along, stop in at **Iris Hantverk** (☏08-21 47 26; Kungsgatan 55; ⏰10am-8pm Mon-Fri, to 3pm Sat) for gorgeous handmade Swedish crafts. Across the street is **WESC** (☏08-21 25 15; www.wesc.com; Kungsgatan 66; ⏰11am-6pm Mon-Fri, 10am-4pm Sat; Ⓜ Hötorget), another museum-like store carrying skateboard-inspired fashion.

E

Humlegården

F

Kungliga
Biblioteket

Engelbrektsplan

vid Bagares Gata

unnsgatan

10 ⊗ Norrlandsgatan

22 🔒

ungsgatan

Sturegatan

Brahegatan

Grev Turegatan

Humlegårdsgatan

Sturestan

ÖSTERMALM

Biblioteksgatan

Birger Jarlsgatan

M Östermalmstorg

äster Samuelsgatan

Smålandsgatan

Norrmalmstorg ⊙
Norrmalmstorg
Hamngatan

🔒 24

gsträd-
gården
M

Vastra Trädgårdsgatan

Kungsträdgården

M Kungsträdgården

Jakobs Kyrka

stav
olfs
org

Norrbro

16 ✪

9 ⊗

8 ⊗ Karl XII's
Torg

Strömgatan

Norrström

Strömbron

Hallwylska
Museet
⊙ 1

Berzelii
Park

14 ⊗

Raoul
Wallenbergs
Torg

Ostermalmstorg

Sibyllegatan

M Östermalmstorg
Östermalmstorg

Storgatan

Sibyllegatan

Dramatiska
teatern

Riddargatan

⊙ Nybroplan

Nybroviken

Tram Line 7

Nybrokajen

Strandvägen

Ladugårdslandsviken

Djurgårdsfärjan Ferry (Summer Only)

6 ⊗
7 ⊗ Grand Hôtel
Stockholm

Museiparken

N   0 ————————— 200 m
    0 ————————— 0.1 miles

Sights

Hallwylska Museet
MUSEUM

1 Map p40, F3

A private palace completed in 1898, Hallwylska Museet was once home to compulsive hoarder Wilhelmina von Hallwyl, who collected items as diverse as kitchen utensils, Chinese pottery, 17th-century paintings, silverware, sculpture and her children's teeth. In 1920 she and her husband donated the mansion and its contents to the state. Guided tours (Skr100, including admission) in English take place at 12.30pm Tuesday to Sunday June through August (weekends only the rest of the year). The museum is not wheelchair accessible. (Hallwyl Collection; ☑08-402 30 99; www.hallwylskamuseet.se; Hamngatan 4; adult/child Skr80/free; ☉10am-4pm Tue-Sun; Ⓜ Östermalmstorg)

Konstakademien
MUSEUM

2 Map p40, D5

While the Nationalmuseum is closed for renovations (set to reopen in 2017), highlights and temporary exhibitions from the collection will be displayed here, in the smaller but very lovely Konstakademien building. The museum has thousands of works to choose from, including painting and sculpture, design objects, prints and drawings from late medieval to current times, so the temporary space is well worth looking into. (Royal Academy of Fine Arts; ☑08-23 29 25; www.konstakad-emien.se; Fredsgatan 12; adult/child Skr100/free; ☉10am-6pm, to 8pm Tue & Thu)

Medelhavsmuseet
MUSEUM

3 Map p40, D5

Housed in an elegant Italianate building, Medelhavsmuseet lures history buffs with its Egyptian, Greek, Cypriot, Roman and Etruscan artefacts. Swoon over sumptuous Islamic art and check out the gleaming gold room, home to a 4th-century-BC olive wreath made of gold. There's also a well-regarded cafe (open 11.30am to 1.30pm). (Museum of Mediterranean Antiquities; ☑010-456 12 98; www.medelhavsmuseet.se; Fredsgatan 2; adult/child Skr80/free; ☉noon-8pm Tue-Fri, to 5pm Sat & Sun; Ⓜ Centralen, Kungsträdgården)

Dansmuseet
MUSEUM

4 Map p40, D5

Having relocated onto a heavily trafficked pedestrian shopping street and added a chic cafe, Dansmuseet (or the Rolf de Maré Dance Museum, after its founder) focuses on the intersections between dance, art and theatre. Collection highlights include traditional dance masks from Africa, India and Tibet; avant-garde costumes from the Russian ballet, Chinese and Japanese theatre puppets; and one of the finest collections of early 20th-century Ballets Russes costumes. (☑08-441 76 51; www.dansmuseet.se; Drottninggatan 17; adult/child Skr60/free; ☉11am-5pm Tue-Sun; Ⓜ Centralen)

Dansmuseet

Kulturhuset

ARTS CENTRE

5 ⊙ Map p40, D4

This architecturally divisive building, opened in 1974, is an arts hub, with a couple of galleries and workshops, a cinema, three restaurants, and libraries containing international periodicals, newspapers, books and an unusually good selection of graphic novels in many languages. Mainly, though, it's home to Stadsteatern (the City Theater), with dance and theatre performances in various-sized venues (mostly in Swedish). The 5th-floor Cafe Panorama has good meals and a stellar view. (✆tickets noon-5pm 08-50 62 02 00; www.kulturhusetstadsteatern.se; Sergels Torg; ⏱11am-5pm, some sections closed Mon; ♿; ☒52, 56, 59, 69, 91 Sergels Torg, ⓂT-Centralen, ☒7 Sergels Torg)

Eating

Grands Verandan

SWEDISH $$$

6 ✕ Map p40, F5

Head here, inside the Grand Hôtel, for the famous smörgåsbord – especially during the Christmas holidays, when it becomes even more elaborate (reservations recommended). Arrive early for a window seat and tuck into both hot and cold Swedish staples, including gravlax with almond potatoes, herring, meatballs and lingonberry jam. It's like a belt-busting crash course in classic Nordic flavours. (✆08-679 35 86;

www.grandhotel.se; Södra Blasieholmshamnen 8, Grand Hôtel Stockholm; smörgåsbord Skr445, mains Skr185-275; ⊘noon-3pm & 6-10pm Mon-Fri, 1-4pm & 6-10pm Sat & Sun; Ⓜ Kungsträdgården)

Mathias Dahlgren

INTERNATIONAL $$$

7 Map p40, F5

Celebrity chef Mathias Dahlgren has settled in at the Grand Hôtel with a two-sided restaurant: there's the formal, elegant Matsalen ('Dining Room'), which has been awarded two Michelin stars, and the bistro-style Matbaren ('Food Bar'), boasting its own Michelin star. Both focus on seasonal ingredients, so menus change daily. Reservations are crucial. (⌚08-679 35 84; www.mathiasdahlgren. com; Södra Blasieholmenshamnen 6, Grand Hôtel Stockholm; Matbaren mains Skr145-295, Matsalen 5-/8-course menu Skr1500/1900; ⊘Matbaren noon-2pm Mon-Fri & 6pm-midnight Mon-Sat, Matsalen 7pm-midnight Tue-Sat, both closed mid-Jul–Aug; Ⓜ Kungsträdgården)

Operakällaren

FRENCH, SWEDISH $$$

8 Map p40, E5

Inside Stockholm's show-off Opera House, the century-old Operakällaren is a major gastronomic event. Decadent chandeliers, golden mirrors and exquisitely carved ceilings set the scene for French-meets-fusion adventures like seared scallops with caramel, cauliflower purée, *pata negra* ham and brown-butter emulsion. Book at least two weeks ahead. (⌚08-676 58 00; www.operakallaren.se; Karl XII's Torg 10; tasting menus Skr995-2750; ⊘6-10pm Tue-Sat, closed mid-Jul–mid-Aug)

Bakfickan

SWEDISH $$$

9 Map p40, E5

The small, casual 'hip pocket' of Operakällaren, this comfy restaurant is crammed with opera photographs and deco lampshades. Dexterous old-school waiters serve comforting Swedish *husmanskost*, and the counter seats make it a perfect spot for solo dining. Late at night, rumour has it, this is where the opera singers hang out. (⌚08-676 58 00; www. operakallaren.se; Karl XII's Torg, Opera House; mains Skr170-275; ⊘11.30am-11pm Mon-Fri, noon-10pm Sat; Ⓜ Kungsträdgården)

Pontus!

SWEDISH $$$

10 Map p40, E2

This Östermalm favourite has reconfigured its space, thankfully keeping the beloved library wallpaper and huge round booths in the main dining room. Indulge in set menus (Skr425 to Skr795) or à la carte mains featuring French-influenced treatments of seasonal ingredients – a chanterelle brioche with sorrel and onion, perhaps, or smoked *matjes* herring with new potatoes and egg-yolk confit. (⌚08-54 52 73 00; Brunnsgatan 1; lunch Skr185, dinner mains Skr155-525; ⊘11.30am-2pm & 6-10pm Mon-Fri, 6-10pm Sat, closed Sun; Ⓜ Östermalmstorg)

La Neta

MEXICAN $

11 Map p40, B2

Competition for the title of 'Stockholm's Best Taqueria' is not fierce, but La Neta wins hands down. Fast-food pseudo-Mexican eateries are all over town, but this is the real deal, with homemade corn tortillas, nuanced flavours and zero frills in the dining area (unless you count the bowls of delicious salsa). It's great value for money. (www.laneta.se; Barnhusgatan 2; 1/5 tacos Skr22/95; ☺11am-9pm Mon-Fri, noon-9pm Sat, noon-4pm Sun; ⓂHötorget)

Hötorgshallen

FOOD HALL $

12 Map p40, C3

Located below Filmstaden cinema, Hötorgshallen is Stockholm at its multicultural best, with stalls selling everything from fresh Nordic seafood to fluffy hummus and fragrant teas. Ready-to-eat options include Lebanese spinach parcels, kebabs and vegetarian burgers. For the ultimate feed, squeeze into galley-themed dining nook **Kajsas Fiskrestaurang** for a huge bowl of soulful *fisksoppa* (fish stew) with aioli (Skr95). (Hötorget; ☺10am-6pm Mon-Thu, to 6.30pm Fri, to 6pm Sat, closed Sun; ⓂHötorget)

Vetekatten

CAFE $

13 Map p40, B3

A cardamom-scented labyrinth of cosy nooks, antique furnishings and oil paintings, Vetekatten is not so much a cafe as an institution. Wish back the old days over filling sandwiches, heavenly scrolls and warming cups of tea. (www.vetekatten.se; Kungsgatan 55; pastries from Skr25, salads Skr65-100; ☺7.30am-7.30pm Mon-Fri, 9.30am-5pm Sat & Sun; ⓂHötorget)

Drinking

Berns Salonger

BAR

14 Map p40, F4

A Stockholm institution since 1862, this glitzy entertainment palace remains one of the city's hottest party spots. While the gorgeous ballroom hosts some brilliant live-music gigs, the best of Berns' bars is in the intimate basement, packed with cool creative types, top-notch DJs and projected art-house images. Check the website for a schedule of events; some require advance ticket purchase. (www.berns.se; Berzelii Park; ☺club 11pm-4am Thu-Sat, occasionally Wed & Sun, bar from 5pm daily)

Absolut Icebar

BAR

15 Map p40, B4

It's touristy. Downright gimmicky! And you're utterly intrigued, admit it: a bar built entirely out of ice, where you drink from glasses carved of ice on tables made of ice. The admission price gets you warm booties, mittens, a parka and one drink. Refill drinks cost Skr95. (☎08-50 56 35 20; www.icebarstockholm.se; Vasaplan 4, Nordic 'C'

Understand
Swedish Film & TV

Sweden led the way in the silent-film era with such masterpieces as *Körkarlen* (The Phantom Carriage). In 1967 came Vilgot Sjöman's notorious *I Am Curious – Yellow,* a subtly hilarious sociopolitical film that got more attention outside Sweden for its X rating than its sharp commentary.

Bergman
One man has largely defined modern Swedish cinema to the outside world: Ingmar Bergman. With deeply contemplative films such as *The Seventh Seal, Through a Glass Darkly* and *Persona,* the beret-topped director explored human alienation, the absence of god, the meaning of life, the certainty of death and other light-hearted themes.

Newer Names
More recently, the Swedish towns of Trollhättan and Ystad have become filmmaking centres, the former drawing the likes of director Lukas Moodysson, whose *Lilja 4-Ever, Show Me Love* and *Tillsammans* were popular and critical hits. Moodysson went through a dark phase for a few years but has found himself back on the international-cinema radar with his newest film, 2014's *We Are the Best!,* an uplifting movie about three high-school girls in 1980s Stockholm who form a punk band out of spite.

Dragon Tattoo
The film version of Stieg Larsson's runaway hit novel, *The Girl with the Dragon Tattoo* (2009), stars Michael Nyqvist and Noomi Rapace and was a huge commercial success. The first instalment in Larsson's series has been remade in English by director David Fincher, with Daniel Craig as journalist Mikael Blomkvist, mostly on location in Sweden.

TV
The Bridge, an excellent Danish-Swedish co-production that has also had an American remake, is a bit grisly. But the unconventional police procedural reveals subtleties of Swedish life that are often overlooked, things like inter-Scandinavian tensions, sexual politics, treatment of minorities and immigrants, and not least, a certain particularly Scandinavian visual style.

Hotel; prebooked online/drop in Skr185/195; ⏲11.15am-midnight Sun-Thu, to 1am Fri & Sat)

Entertainment

Operan OPERA

 16 Map p40, E5

The Royal Opera is the place to go for thunderous tenors, sparkling sopranos and classical ballet. It has some bargain tickets in seats with poor views, and occasional lunchtime concerts for less than Skr200 (including light lunch). (☑08-791 44 00; www.operan.se; Gustav Adolfs Torg, Operahuset; tickets Skr100-750; ⓂKungsträdgården)

Fasching JAZZ

17 Map p40, B3

Music club Fasching is the pick of Stockholm's jazz clubs, with live music most nights. DJs take over with either Afrobeat, Latin, neo-soul or R&B on Friday night and retro-soul, disco and rare grooves on Saturday. (☑08-53 48 29 60; www.fasching.se; Kungsgatan 63; ⏲6pm-1am Mon-Thu, to 4am Fri & Sat, 5pm-1am Sun; ⓂT-Centralen)

Glenn Miller Café JAZZ, BLUES

18 Map p40, D2

Simply loaded with character, this tiny jazz-and-blues bar draws a faithful, fun-loving evening crowd. It also serves excellent, affordable French-style classics like mussels with white wine sauce. (☑08-10 03 22;

Brunnsgatan 21A; ⏲5pm-1am Mon-Thu, to 2am Fri & Sat)

Konserthuset CLASSICAL MUSIC

 19 Map p40, C2

Head to this pretty blue building for classical concerts and other musical marvels, including the Royal Philharmonic Orchestra. (☑08-50 66 77 88; www.konserthuset.se; Hötorget; tickets Skr80-325; ⓂHötorget)

Stockholms Stadsteatern THEATRE

20 Map p40, D4

Regular performances are staged at this theatre inside Kulturhuset, as well as guest appearances by foreign theatre companies. (☑08-50 62 02 00; www.stadsteatern.stockholm.se; Kulturhuset, Sergels Torg; tickets Skr200-350; ⓂT-Centralen)

Dansens Hus DANCE

21 Map p40, B2

This place is an absolute must for contemporary-dance fans. Guest artists to have performed here have included everyone from British choreographer Akram Khan to Canadian innovator Daniel Léveillé. (☑08-50 89 90 90; www.dansenshus.se; Barnhusgatan 12-14; tickets around Skr300, under 20yr half-price)

Understand

Swedish Design

You don't have to spend much time window-shopping in this city to realise that Stockholm is a living museum of contemporary design. There are zero unstyled objects – no ordinary anything. From milk cartons by Tom Hedqvist to ballerina 'tutu' lamps by Jonas Bohlin, the everyday things you see around you here are object lessons in style and innovation.

Democratic Design

This is, after all, the birthplace of democratic design behemoth IKEA, and that concept did not spring out of nowhere. Great design is meant to be a part of ordinary life in Sweden, from the living room to the nightclub.

The influence of IKEA has been enormous – it has sought to bring simple, good design to the whole world, affordably. Cheap and innovative designs were born of Swedish modern design – the idea of the house as the starting point of good design, rather than the end.

Where to Find It

There are many ways to immerse yourself in Swedish design and gain an appreciation for its history. One is simply to walk around the city with your eyes open. But it's also worthwhile to spend some time window-shopping, especially at landmark shops like Svenskt Tenn (p93) and Nordiska Galleriet (p93).

Department stores like NK and PUB are also great sources of the things everyday Swedes furnish their homes with.

For something more like a history lesson, visit Nordiska Museet (p63) and its displays of design objects from throughout Swedish history.

Or make a pilgrimage to some of the sleeker hotels, bars and restaurants in town – Sturehof (p91) was gussied up by Jonas Bohlin, Thomas Sandell did **Café Opera** (☎08-676 58 07; www.cafeopera.se; Karl XII's Torg; admission from Skr160; ☉10pm-3am Wed-Sun; ⓂKungsträdgården), and you can enjoy a smörgåsbord of interior designers at design-focused boutique hotels like the **Birger Jarl Hotel** (☎08-674 18 00; www.birgerjarl.se; Tulegatan 8; cabin r Skr690, s & d from Skr890, studios from Skr1890; P❀❄@☎; ☐43 Tegnérgatan, ⓂRådmansgatan).

Shopping

Naturkompaniet   OUTDOOR EQUIPMENT

22 🔒 Map p40, E2

Find everything you might need for an excursion into the Swedish wilderness here, from backpacks and sleeping bags to woolly socks, headlamps, cooking stoves and compasses. There are several other locations across the city. (www.naturkompaniet.se; Kungsgatan 4; ⏰10am-6.30pm Mon-Fri, 10am-5pm Sat, noon-4pm Sun; Ⓜ Östermalmstorg)

Kartbutiken   MAPS

23 🔒 Map p40, C3

This huge, helpful store has all kinds of maps and guidebooks for Scandinavia and elsewhere, from urban centres to remote hiking areas, plus a variety of gifts and gadgets. (☎08-20 23 03; www.kartbutiken.se; Mäster Samuelsgatan 54; ⏰10am-6pm Mon-Fri, 10am-4pm Sat, noon-4pm Sun; Ⓜ T-Centralen)

NK   DEPARTMENT STORE

24 🔒 Map p40, E3

An ultra-classy department store founded in 1902, NK (Nordiska Kompaniet) is a city landmark – you can see its rotating neon sign from most parts of Stockholm. You'll find top-name brands and several nice cafes, and the basement levels are great for stocking up on souvenirs and gourmet groceries. Around Christmas, check out its inventive window displays. (☎08-762 80 00; www.nk.se; Hamngatan 12-18; ⏰10am-8pm Mon-Fri, 10am-6pm Sat, 11am-5pm Sun; Ⓜ T-Centralen)

PUB   DEPARTMENT STORE

25 🔒 Map p40, C3

Historic department store PUB is best known as the former workplace of Greta Garbo, and advertisements still work that angle pretty strongly. It's a major fashion and lifestyle hub, carrying fresh Nordic labels like Stray Boys, House of Dagmar and Baum & Pferdgarten. Refuel at the slinky cafe-bar. (Drottninggatan 72-6; ⏰10am-7pm Mon-Fri, 10am-6pm Sat, 11am-5pm Sun; Ⓜ Hötorget)

Åhléns   DEPARTMENT STORE

26 🔒 Map p40, C3

For all-in-one retail therapy, scour department-store giant Åhléns. (☎08-676 60 00; Klarabergsgatan 50; ⏰10am-9pm Mon-Fri, 10am-7pm Sat, 11am-7pm Sun; Ⓜ T-Centralen)

Explore

Djurgården & Skeppsholmen

The parklike island of Djurgården is a museum-goer's dream. Not only are many of Stockholm's top museums gathered here, but the setting is sublime: gardens, greenery, a lazy river, cycle paths, picnic places, and all of it just a short bridge away from the centre of town. Neighbouring Skeppsholmen is also home to a couple of major museums, and is connected by a small footbridge to the city centre.

The Sights in a Day

☼ You could easily spend the whole day at **Skansen** (p52) if you wanted, but let's assume you want to hit a few other spots as well. Get to Skansen early, and have a rough plan about which parts of it you most want to see – you'll probably need to pick and choose. Get a snack there before you leave, or stop for a quiet post-Skansen lunch at the **Blå Porten Café** (p66).

☼ Spend the next hour or two in one of the city's best-loved museums, **Vasamuseet** (p56), dedicated to the sunken battleship. If you're travelling as a family, another option is to send the kids to Vasamuseet while the parents check out the excellent **Spritmuseum** (p63), all about the history of booze and vice in Sweden. There's a great cafe there, as well.

☽ If you've planned cleverly, this is a Tuesday or a Friday, which means **Moderna Museet** (p58) is open until 8pm so you can take a leisurely stroll over to it and have plenty of time to look around. Wrap it up with a good meal at the museum's award-winning restaurant.

For a local's day in Djurgården, see p60.

👁 Top Sights

Skansen (p52)

Vasamuseet (p56)

Moderna Museet (p58)

◯ Local Life

Escaping to Djurgården (p60)

💙 Best of Stockholm

Museums & Galleries
Nordiska Museet (p63)

Spritmuseum (p63)

Eating
Rosendals Trädgårdskafe (p67)

For Kids
Skansen (p52)

Junibacken (p64)

Aquaria Vattenmuseum (p64)

Gröna Lund Tivoli (p65)

Getting There

🚌 **Bus** 44, 65, 69

🚃 **Tram** 7 from Norrmalmstorg

⛴ **Djurgårdsfärjan** Ferry services connect Djurgården to Slussen and Skeppsholmen every 10 minutes; SL passes (p149) are valid

Ⓜ **Tunnelbana** Kungsträdgården, T-Centralen

Top Sights
Skansen

The world's first open-air museum and a delight to visit, especially with kids, Skansen was founded in 1891 by Artur Hazelius to give visitors an idea of how Swedes lived once upon a time. You could easily spend a day here and still not see it all. Around 150 traditional houses and other exhibits from across the country cover the hill – it's meant to be 'Sweden in miniature', complete with villages, nature, commerce and industry.

◉ Map p62, D3

www.skansen.se

Djurgårdsvägen

adult/child Skr160/60

🕙10am-10pm late Jun–Aug

🚌44, ⬇Djurgårdsfärjan,
🚋7, Djurgården

Baking bread

Don't Miss

Skansen Zoo

The Skansen Zoo, with moose, reindeer, wolverines, lynx and other native wildlife, is a highlight, especially in spring when baby critters scamper around – the brown bear cubs are irresistible. Around 75 species of Scandinavian animals live in the zoo, along with a few imported species. There's also a petting zoo where young children can meet small animals.

Glassblowers' Workshop

The glassblowers' workshop is a popular stop: watching the intricate forms emerge from glowing blobs of liquid glass is transfixing. The shop was moved here from a Slussen basement in 1936 – the craftswoman in charge today is the third generation of that same original family. If you're wondering, the temperature of the oven is 1130°C (2066°F).

Rescued Buildings

Within Skansen, there's a still-working bakery, a bank and post office, a machine shop, botanical gardens and Hazelius' mansion. Part of the pharmacy was moved here from Drottningholm castle; two little garden huts came from Tantolunden, a community garden still operating in Södermalm. There's also a Sami camp, farmsteads representing several regions, a manor house and a school.

Music & Events

Daily activities take place on Skansen's stages, including folk dancing and an enormous public festival at Midsummer's Eve (first Friday after 19 June). If you're in Stockholm for any of the country's major celebrations, such as Walpurgis Night (30 April) or St Lucia Day (13 December), it's a

☑ Top Tips

▶ Prices and hours vary seasonally and closing times for each workshop can vary, so check times online to avoid disappointment.

▶ From mid-June through August, Waxholmsbolaget (www.waxholmsbolaget.se) ferries run from Slussen to Djurgården; the route is part of the regular SL transit system, so you can use your SL pass to board. It's about a five-minute trip and runs every 10 minutes or so.

▶ A map and an excellent booklet in English are available to guide you.

▶ It's not cheating to take the escalator to the top of the hill and meander down from there.

✗ Take a Break

Just outside the Skansen gates you'll find the lovely Blå Porten Café (p66), with simple meals in a garden setting. For something a little more formal, look into Wärdshuset Ulla Winbladh (p67).

popular place to watch Swedes celebrate. In summer, check out Allsång, a televised sing-along on Skansen's main stage.

Aquarium

The **Skansen Aquarium** (Akvariet; adult/child Skr100/60) is worth a wander, its residents including piranhas, lemurs and pygmy marmosets (the smallest monkeys in the world). Intrepid visitors may be allowed into the cages of some of the animals – check the daily schedule posted at Skansen's main gate. (Unlike most museums inside Skansen, the aquarium has a separate admission fee.)

Tobaks & Tändsticksmuseum

Inside Skansen you'll find the Tobaks & Tändsticksmuseum, which traces the history and culture of smoking and the manufacture of those iconic Swedish matches. You won't be long in Sweden without seeing *snus* – here

you can learn its history and how to mix your own blend. The museum also hosts occasional cigar tastings; check schedules on the Skansen website.

Biologiska Museet

As notable for its creaky wooden building as for its collection of critters, the 1893 Biologiska museet charms visitors with two circular floors of stuffed wildlife in nature dioramas. It's fun checking the numbered keys to identify some of the more unusual specimens in their various habitats, and the dioramas and backgrounds are remarkably realistic.

Vastveit Storehouse

There's a top-heavy little wooden hut at the far northern side of Skansen – called Vastveit, it's a storehouse that was imported from Norway, and is reportedly the oldest building in the park, with parts of it dating from the 14th century. The shape is typical of traditional Swedish mountain and farmstead huts; many are still in use.

Dalahäst

Look for the giant wooden *Dalahäst*, a favourite photo op for smaller kids. You'll find it and other playground equipment on Orsakullen, an open area right in the centre of Skansen, which is also conveniently near some restrooms and snack kiosks. *Dalahästar* (souvenir wooden horses) in more portable sizes can be found in the main Skansen gift shop (and all over town).

Understand

Living History

Buildings in the open-air museum represent various trades and areas of industry from Sweden's earliest days. In most of them you'll find staff dressed up in period costume, often making crafts, playing music or churning butter while cheerfully answering questions about the folk whose lives they're re-creating. It's a potentially silly conceit, but charming in this setting.

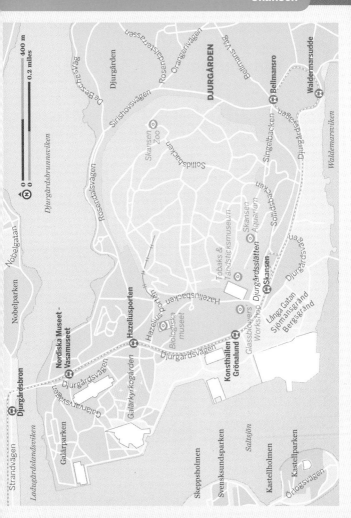

Top Sights
Vasamuseet

A good-humoured glorification of some dodgy calculations, Vasamuseet is the custom-built home of the massive warship *Vasa*. The ship, a whopping 69m long and 48.8m tall, was the pride of the Swedish crown when it set off on its maiden voyage on 10 August 1628. Within minutes, the top-heavy vessel tipped and sank to the bottom of Saltsjön, along with many of the people on board. The museum details its painstaking retrieval and restoration, as well as putting the whole thing into historical context.

Map p18, B2

www.vasamuseet.se

Galärvarvsvägen 14

adult/child Skr130/free

8.30am-6pm

44, Djurgårdsfärjan, 7 Nordiska museet/Vasa

Don't Miss

Exhibits

Five levels of exhibits cover artefacts salvaged from the *Vasa*, life on board, naval warfare and 17th-century sailing and navigation, plus sculptures and temporary exhibitions. The bottom-floor exhibition is particularly fascinating, using modern forensic science to re-create the faces and life stories of several of the ill-fated passengers. The ship was painstakingly raised in 1961 and reassembled like a giant 14,000-piece jigsaw. Almost all of what you see today is original.

Meanwhile

Putting the catastrophic fate of the *Vasa* in historical context is a permanent multimedia exhibit, *Meanwhile*. With images of events and moments happening simultaneously around the globe – from China to France to 'New Amsterdam', from traders and settlers to royal families to working mothers and put-upon merchants – it establishes a vivid setting for the story at hand.

Scale Model

On the entrance level is a model of the ship at scale 1:10, painted according to a thoroughly researched understanding of how the original would've looked. Once you've studied it, look for the intricately carved decorations adorning the actual *Vasa*. The stern in particular is gorgeous – it was badly damaged but has been slowly and carefully restored.

Upper Deck

A reconstruction of the upper gun deck allows visitors to get a feel for what it might have been like to be on a vessel this size. The *Vasa* had two gun decks, which held an atypically large number of cannons – thought to be part of the reason it capsized.

☑ Top Tips

▶ Guided tours in English depart from the front entrance every 30 minutes in summer.

▶ Near the entrance of the museum is a cinema screening a 25-minute film covering topics not included in the exhibitions (in English at 9.30am and 1.30pm daily in summer).

▶ You can climb aboard the reconstructed upper gun deck but the actual ship is off-limits for its safety.

✕ Take a Break

There's a restaurant inside the museum, serving coffee, drinks and full meals. Outside the museum, you're not far from Blå Porten Café (p66) and its outdoor garden seating, or the more formal Wärdshuset Ulla Winbladh (p67), which also has inviting outdoor seating areas.

Top Sights
Moderna Museet

Moderna Museet is Stockholm's modern-art maverick, with a world-class permanent collection of paintings, sculpture, photography, video art and installations. Highlights include work by Pablo Picasso, Salvador Dalí, Andy Warhol and Damien Hirst – as well as their Scandinavian contemporaries, and plenty of work by not-yet-household names.

The museum also stages well-conceived temporary exhibits and career retrospectives (sometimes with a separate admission fee), often focused on Scandinavian artists.

Map p18, A3

www.modernamuseet.se

Exercisplan 4

adult/child Skr120/free, 6-8pm Fri free

10am-6pm Wed, Thu, Sat & Sun, to 8pm Tue & Fri

65, Djurgårdsfärjan

Outdoor sculptures

Don't Miss

First Gallery: 1900 to 1940s

The galleries on the museum's main floor are arranged by era, aside from the large space used for temporary exhibitions. In the first of the permanent collection's three rooms, you'll find early modernists like Edvard Munch and Ernst Ludwig Kirchner. Look for Georgio de Chirico's *The Child's Brain* and several pieces by Marcel Duchamp.

Second Gallery: Post-War to 1970s

The middle gallery on the main floor holds the most familiar names: you'll find Francis Bacon's portrait of Lucian Freud; an enormous and exuberant Henri Matisse cut-out, *Apollo*, covering one whole wall; Salvador Dalí; Georges Braque; and Pablo Picasso. This is also where you'll find Robert Rauschenberg's best-known 'combine', a 1959 piece consisting of a taxidermied goat painted and stuck through the middle of a tyre, over a collage.

Third Gallery: 1970s to the Present

The third room holds the newest additions to the permanent collection, and as such is the most frequently changing. Things you might find here include Barbara Kruger paintings, Donald Judd installations, and envelope-pushing work by people most of us haven't heard of yet.

Outdoor Sculptures

Arranged on the grounds around the museum are several sculptures by a wide variety of artists. The most attention-grabbing are the large colourful figures by Niki di Saint Phalle and Jean Tinguely, called *The Fantastic Paradise*. There's also an Alexander Calder and a Picasso, and work by several Swedish sculptors in the walled sculpture garden.

☑ Top Tips

▶ Admission is free 6pm to 8pm Fridays.

▶ Note that the museum is closed on Mondays.

▶ Keep in mind that the permanent collection is rearranged frequently, and items from the collection are loaned out to other museums now and then.

✕ Take a Break

There's a fabulous and very popular **restaurant** (daily lunch Skr120; ⏱11am-2pm) with a great view over the water; an espresso bar in the foyer (next to the heavenly bookstore); and a small, casual **cafe** (salads & sandwiches Skr115-125) in a nice secluded courtyard.

Local Life
Escaping to Djurgården

In a perfect world, every city would have a place like Djurgården, a quiet, leafy green retreat from the noise and traffic of the working world. It is literally steps away from the heart of downtown Stockholm, but the park island feels like an otherworldly oasis. Part is occupied by Skansen and other excellent museums, but most consists of quiet trails through fields and forests, where locals exercise, picnic or just wander around.

❶ Blue Gate

As soon as you walk across the bridge (Djurgårdsbron) from Norrmalm to Djurgården, you'll see a huge, bright-blue wrought-iron gate to your left. Go ahead and walk through it, and you'll be on the footpath alongside Djurgårdsbrunnsviken, the long stretch of water that separates Djurgården from Ladugårdsgärdet to the north. Stay on the trail along the water's edge, stopping to admire

baby ducks and passing boats as they appear.

2 Rosendal

Eventually you'll reach signs pointing you toward **Rosendals Slott** (☎08-402 61 30; www.kungahuset.se; Rosendals-vägen 49; adult/child Skr100/free; ◷hourly noon-3pm Tue-Sun Jun-Aug; ◻44, 69, ◻7). Rosendal was built as a palace for Karl XIV Johan in the 1820s. One of Sweden's finest examples of the Empire style, it sparkles with sumptuous royal furnishings. Admission is by guided tour only – but even just the setting is well worth going to, and it's a handy landmark to orient yourself on the island.

3 Botanical Gardens

The *trädgård* (botanical gardens) attached to Rosendals Slott are well worth a look. They're designed as a forum for educating the public on the techniques and possibilities of organic gardening, but they're also just fun to wander through. You'll see everything from herbs and roses to vegetables and wine grapes – and of course an organic compost heap. King Oscar I built the orangery in 1848.

4 Biskopsudden

This area sticks out a bit from the main island, which means it has excellent views across the water of the surrounding parts of Stockholm. There's a little cafe by the marina,

Cafe Ekorren (www.cafeekorren.se; Biskopsvägen 5; daily lunch Skr98, mains Skr165-185; ◷10am-7pm, ◻47, 69), with outdoor tables beside the water as well as a little yellow hut for indoor seating. It's a great place to kick your feet up for a while and have a coffee or an ice cream. (Full meals are also available.)

5 Waldemarsudde Garden Trails

The grounds around the highly recommended **Waldemarsudde gallery** (☎08-54 58 37 07; www.waldemarsudde.com; Prins Eugens väg 6; adult/child Skr100/free; ◷11am-5pm Tue-Sun, to 8pm Thu, gardens 8am-9pm; ◻7) are equally well worth a visit – they're beautifully arranged, with multiple levels of walking paths and unexpected waterside gazebos that provide any number of picturesque views from different vantage points. Prins Eugen's grave is here, in a small, peaceful copse. Bring your camera and explore.

6 Estonia Monument

As you wander back toward the bridge where the walk began, you'll pass the busy museums around Skansen. Take a small detour to visit the Estonia Monument. The structure was built to commemorate the ferry disaster of 28 September 1994, in which 852 people drowned when a boat en route from Tallinn capsized in stormy weather.

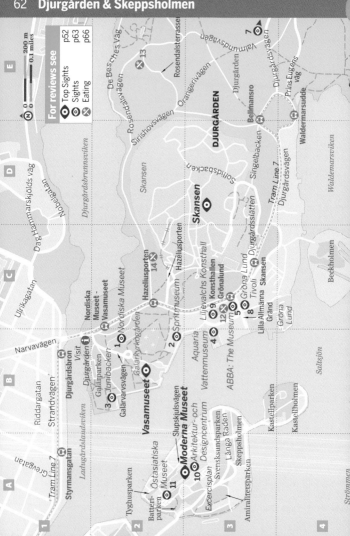

0   200 m
0   0.1 miles

De Beches Väg
Rosendalsterrassen
Valmundsvägen
7
Orangerivägen
Djurgården
Djurgårdsvägen
Rosendalsvägen
Sirishovsvägen
Prins Eugens väg
13
DJURGÅRDEN
Bellmansro
Waldemarsudde
Nobelgatan
Dag Hammarskjölds väg
Djurgårdsbrunnsviken
Skansen
Sollidsbacken
Singelbacken
Waldemarsviken
Ulrikagatan
Solidsbacken
Skansen
Tram Line 7
Djurgårdsvägen
Beckholmen
Hazeliusporten
Hazeliusporten
Konsthallen
Djurgårdsslätten
14
Nordiska Museet
Hazeliusporten
Lilievalchs Konsthall
Gröna Lund
Skansen
Narvavägen
Nordiska
Museet -
Vasamuseet
Spritmuseum
9
Gröna Lund
Saltsjön
Djurgårdsbron
Visit
Djurgårdsbron
Galärparken
Nordiska Museet
1
Galärkyrkogården
2
Aquaria
Vattenmuseum
12
5
Lilla Allmänna
Gränd
Gröna
Lund
Tivoli
8
Riddargatan
Strandvägen
Galärvarvsvägen
Junibacken
Galärparken
Vasamuseet
ABBA: The Museum
Kastellparken
Kastellholmen
Styrmansgatan
3
Galärvarvsvägen
Vasamuseet
Slupskjulsvägen
Arkitektur- och
Designcentrum
Kastellholmen
Grevgatan
Tram Line 7
Ladugårdslandsviken
Tyghusparken
Moderna Museet
10
Svensksundsvägen
Långa Raden
Skeppsholmen
Strömmen
Batteri-
parken
Östasiatiska
Museet
11
Excercisplan
Amiralitetsparken

Spritmuseum

Sights

Nordiska Museet
MUSEUM

1 ◉ Map p62, B2

The epic Nordiska Museet is Sweden's largest cultural-history museum and one of its largest indoor spaces. The building itself (from 1907) is an eclectic, Renaissance-style castle designed by Isak Gustav Clason, who also drew up Östermalms Saluhall. Inside you'll find a sprawling collection of all things Swedish, from sacred Sami objects to fashion, shoes, home interiors and even table settings. (☑08-51 95 47 70; www.nordiskamuseet.se; Djurgårdsvägen 6-16; adult/child Skr100/free; ☉10am-5pm; ☒44, 69, ☒Djurgårdsfärjan, ☒7)

Spritmuseum
MUSEUM

2 ◉ Map p62, B2

The surprisingly entertaining Museum of Spirits is dedicated to Sweden's complicated relationship with alcohol, as mediated over the years by the state-run monopoly System Bolaget. The slick space, in two 18th-century naval buildings, covers the history, manufacture and consumption of all kinds of booze, plus holiday traditions, drinking songs, food pairings and so on. Best of all, you can combine your visit with a tasting kit (Skr200), including various flavours of liquor to be sampled at specified points. (Museum of Spirits; ☑08-12 13 13 00; www. spritmuseum.se; Djurgårdsvägen 38;

admission Skr100; ⊙10am-5pm, to 8pm Tue; 🚌44, 69, 🚢Djurgårdsfärjan, 🚋7)

Junibacken AMUSEMENT PARK

3 ◉ Map p62, B2

Junibacken whimsically recreates the fantasy scenes of Astrid Lindgren's books for children. Catch the flying Story Train over Stockholm, shrink to the size of a sugar cube, and end up at Villekulla cottage, where kids can shout, squeal and dress up like Pippi Longstocking. The bookshop is a treasure trove of children's books, as well as a great place to pick up anything from cheeky Karlsson dolls to cute little art cards with story-book themes. (www.junibacken.se; Djurgården; adult/child Skr145/125; ⊙10am-5pm or 6pm; 👶; 🚌44, 69, 🚢Djurgårdsfärjan, 🚋7)

Aquaria Vattenmuseum MUSEUM

4 ◉ Map p62, B3

This conservation-themed aquarium, complete with seahorses, sharks, piranhas and clownfish, takes you through a range of environmental zones – from tropical jungle and coral reef to sewer systems – with an emphasis on ecology and the fragility of the marine environment. If that sounds a bit of a drag, it's not – there's enough to do and see to keep the family entertained. Time your visit to coincide with a feeding, daily at 11am, 1.30pm and 2.30pm. (☎08-660 90 89; www.aquaria.se; Falkenbergsgatan 2; adult/ child Skr130/85; ⊙10am-4.30pm Tue-Sun; 👶; 🚌44, 69, 🚢Djurgårdsfärjan, 🚋7)

ABBA: The Museum MUSEUM

5 ◉ Map p62, C3

A sensory-overload experience that might appeal only to devoted Abba fans, this long-awaited and wildly hyped cathedral to the demigods of Swedish pop is almost aggressively entertaining. It's packed to the gills with memorabilia and interactivity – every square inch has something new to look at, be it a glittering guitar, a vintage photo of Benny, Björn, Frida or Agnetha, a classic music video, an outlandish costume or a tour van from the band members' early days. (☎08-12 13 28 60; www.abbathemuseum.com; Djurgårdsvägen 68; adult/child Skr195/50; ⊙10am-8pm, shorter hours in winter; 🚌44, 🚢Djurgårdsfärjan, 🚋7)

Prins Eugens Waldemarsudde MUSEUM

6 ◉ Map p62, E4

Prins Eugens Waldemarsudde, at the southern tip of Djurgården, is a soul-perking combo of water views and art. The palace once belonged to the painter prince (1865–1947), who favoured art over typical royal pleasures. In addition to Eugen's own work, it holds his impressive collection of Nordic paintings and sculptures, including works by Anders Zorn and Carl Larsson. The buildings and galleries, connected by tunnels, are surrounded by soothing gardens (free to wander) and an old windmill from the 1780s. (☎08-54 58 37 07; www.waldemarsudde.com; Prins Eugens väg 6; adult/child Skr100/free;

Gröna Lund Tivoli

🕙11am-5pm Tue-Sun, to 8pm Thu, gardens 8am-9pm; 🚌7)

Thielska Galleriet GALLERY

7 ◎ Map p62, E3

Thielska Galleriet, at the far eastern end of Djurgården, is a must for Nordic art fans, with a savvy collection of late 19th- and early 20th-century works from Scandinavian greats like Carl Larsson, Anders Zorn, Ernst Josephson and Bruno Liljefors, plus a series of Edvard Munch's etchings of vampiric women and several paintings from a bridge you'll recognise from *The Scream*. (Ernest Thiel, a banker and translator, was one of Munch's patrons.) Free tours in English happen at 2pm Friday in sum-

mer. (🕿08-662 58 84; www.thielska-galleriet. se; Sjötullsbacken 8; adult/child Skr100/free; 🕙noon-5pm Tue-Sun; 🚌69)

Gröna Lund Tivoli AMUSEMENT PARK

8 ◎ Map p62, C3

Crowded Gröna Lund Tivoli has some 30 rides, ranging from the tame (a German circus carousel) to the terrifying (the Free Fall, where you drop from a height of 80m in six seconds after glimpsing a lovely, if brief, view over Stockholm). There are countless places to eat and drink in the park, but whether you'll keep anything down is another matter entirely. The Åkband day pass gives unlimited rides, or individual rides range from Skr20 to Skr60. (www.

gronalund.com; Lilla Allmänna gränd 9; adult/child under 7yr Skr110/free, unlimited ride pass Skr310; ⏱10am-11pm summer, shorter hours rest of year; ♿; 🚌44, 🚢Djurgårdsfärjan, 🚋7)

Liljevalchs Konsthall · GALLERY

9 Map p62, C3

Opened in 1916, Liljevalchs puts on at least four major exhibitions a year of contemporary Swedish and international art, including the popular Spring Salon. (☎08-50 83 13 30; www.liljevalchs.se; Djurgårdsvägen 60; adult/child Skr80/free; ⏱11am-5pm Jun-Aug, shorter hours rest of year; 🚌44, 69, 🚢Djurgårdsfärjan, 🚋7)

Arkitektur- och Designcentrum · MUSEUM

10 Map p62, A3

Adjoining Moderna Museet and housed in a converted navy drill hall, the architecture and design centre has a permanent exhibition spanning 1000 years of Swedish architecture and an archive of 2.5 million documents, photographs, plans, drawings and models. Temporary exhibitions also cover international names and work. The museum organises occasional themed architectural tours of Stockholm; check the website or ask at the information desk. (☎08-58 72 70 00; www.arkdes.se; Exercisplan 4; adult/child Skr80/free, 4-6pm Fri free, combination ticket with Moderna Museet Skr180; ⏱10am-8pm Tue, to 6pm Wed-Sun; 🚌65, 🚢Djurgårdsfärjan)

Östasiatiska Museet · MUSEUM

11 Map p62, A2

This long, narrow building displays Asian decorative arts, including one of the world's finest collections of Chinese stoneware and porcelain from the Sing, Ming and Qing dynasties. The museum also houses the largest and oldest Asian library in Scandinavia, from which several notable specimens are displayed. The often refreshing temporary exhibitions cover a wide range of themes, with past shows including a look at Japanese anime characters and Chinese video art. (Museum of Far Eastern Antiquities; www.ostasiatiska.se; Tyghusplan; adult/child Skr80/free; ⏱11am-8pm Tue, to 5pm Wed-Sun; 🚌65)

Eating

Blå Porten Café · CAFE $$

12 Map p62, C3

Blissful on sunny days, when you can linger over lunch or *fika* (the daily coffee ritual) in a garden reminiscent of a Monet painting, this cafe next to Liljevalchs Konsthall boasts an obscenely tempting display of baked goods, as well as lip-smacking Scandi and global meals. Mercifully, many of Djurgården's museums are within rolling distance. (☎08-663 87 59; www.blaporten.com; Djurgårdsvägen 64; mains Skr85-155; ⏱11am-9pm Mon-Thu, to 7pm Fri-Sun; 🖋; 🚌47 Liljevalc Gröna Lund, 🚋7 Liljevalc Gröna Lund)

Blå Porten Café

Rosendals Trädgårdskafe
CAFE $$

13   Map p62, E2

Set among the greenhouses of a pretty botanical garden (p61), Rosendals is an idyllic spot for heavenly pastries and coffee or a meal and a glass of organic wine. Lunch includes a brief menu of ecofriendly soups, sandwiches (such as ground-lamb burger with chanterelles) and gorgeous salads. Much of the produce is biodynamic and grown on-site. (☎08-54 58 12 70; www.rosendalstradgard.se; Rosendalsterrassen 12; mains Skr85-145; ☺11am-5pm Mon-Fri, to 6pm Sat & Sun May-Sep, closed Mon Feb-Apr & Oct-Dec; Ⓟ🅰; 🚌44, 69, 76 Djurgårdsbron, 🚋7)

Wärdshuset Ulla Winbladh
SWEDISH $$$

14   Map p62, C2

Named after one of Carl Michael Bellman's lovers, this villa was built as a steam bakery for the Stockholm World's Fair (1897) and now serves fine food in intimate rooms and a blissful garden setting. Sup on skilfully prepared upscale versions of traditional Scandi favourites, mostly built around fish and potatoes – try the herring plate with homemade crispbread. (☎08-53 48 97 01; www.ullawinbladh.se; Rosendalsvägen 8; starters Skr125-265, mains Skr155-295; ☺11.30am-10pm Mon, 11.30am-11pm Tue-Fri, 12.30-11pm Sat, 12.30-10pm Sun; 🚢Djurgårdsfärjan, 🚋7)

Explore

Södermalm

You know you've arrived when a cultural behemoth like *Vogue* magazine declares you the third-coolest neighbourhood in the entire world. Södermalm lives up to the hype, at least if you know where to look – certain corners of it are almost intimidatingly cool, though of course it's also just a regular neighbourhood where people live and work.

The Sights in a Day

☼ Though known for its nightlife, Södermalm is also home to some great family-friendly museums. Start with a visit to **Stockholms Stadsmuseum** (p76), which provides an immersive experience that will give you a good sense of the city's shape, structure and development over the years.

☼ Stop for some refreshments, perhaps a veggie lunch at **Chutney** (p77) – an excellent-value and very cosy little cafe. Then hop a bus toward two museums in the same building, **Leksaksmuseet** (p76) and **Spårvägsmuseet** (p76), for a primer on toys and transportation respectively.

☾ Make your way back toward Slussen to check out **Fotografiska** (p70), which stays open relatively late. By then, you've earned a beer: stroll over and choose from the vast selection of brews at **Akkurat** (p80).

For a local's night in Södermalm, see p72.

◉ **Top Sights**

Fotografiska (p70)

◯ **Local Life**

Södermalm Bar-Hopping (p72)

♥ **Best of Stockholm**

Eating

Chutney (p77)

Hermans Trädgårdscafé (p76)

Drinking

Pet Sounds Bar (p79)

Akkurat (p80)

For Kids

Spårvägsmuseet (p76)

Leksaksmuseet (p76)

Music

Debaser (p72)

Mosebacke Etablissement (p81)

Getting There

Ⓜ **Tunnelbana** Slussen, Medborgarplatsen, Zinkensdamm

Top Sights
Fotografiska

A chic, upmarket photography museum, Fotografiska is a must for shutterbugs. Its temporary exhibitions are huge, interestingly chosen and well presented; examples have included a Robert Mapplethorpe retrospective and portraits by indie filmmaker Gus Van Sant. The museum draws around 500,000 visitors a year and offers photography courses, as well as staging occasional concerts and other one-off events. And it has one of the coolest locations in Stockholm.

Map p18, G2

www.fotografiska.eu

Stadsgårdshamnen 22

adult/child Skr120/90

🕑9am-9pm Sun-Wed, to 11pm Thu-Sat

Ⓜ Slussen

Don't Miss

Permanent Collection
The museum serves as a photo archive as well as an exhibition hall; it is home to a strong permanent collection of photos from international and Scandinavian photographers. Brothers Jan and Per Broman launched the museum in 2010, though discussions about such a project had been happening since the 1940s.

Temporary Exhibitions
In addition to its permanent collection, the museum holds four major temporary exhibitions a year, often in the form of retrospectives of big-name artists, as well as 15 to 20 smaller temporary exhibits. One recent show featured an enormous collection of black-and-white photos by Sebastião Salgado. Others have included the likes of Annie Leibovitz, David LaChapelle, Klara Kallstrom and Johan Wik. They're usually accompanied by extensive, sophisticated information in English.

The Building
Fotografiska is housed in a massive (5500 sq metre) industrial art-nouveau brick structure designed by the well-known architect Ferdinand Boberg and built in 1906. It was originally a customs hall, and underwent a Skr250 million renovation to transform the interior for the museum, while keeping the original brick facade.

Gift Shop
Plan to spend some time browsing the gift shop, as it's a particularly well stocked one. The collection of eccentric little cameras alone is interesting, but there are also hundreds of photos available to purchase and, of course, photography books, postcards, posters and so on.

☑ Top Tips
▸ Follow signs from the Slussen tunnelbana station along the waterfront to reach the museum.

✗ Take a Break
In the summer months, the terrace in front of the museum entrance becomes Grill, a lively bar and cafe serving cocktails and a brief menu of dinner specials and filling salads, usually with pumping DJ music in the background. The cafe on the museum's top floor serves coffee and cakes, decadent sandwiches and salads year-round, and the view from its panoramic windows is breathtaking.

Ready to leave the museum? Climb the stairs behind the building to Hermans Trädgårdskafe (p76) for a veggie buffet with a view.

Local Life
Södermalm Bar-Hopping

It's a well-established fact that any neighbourhood where artists and bohemian types live and work is a good place for a bar hop. In Stockholm, Söder is that neighbourhood, and the bars range from comfy dives to beautifully designed jewel boxes. The unifying factor, even in the coolest bars, is an unfussy open-mindedness. This part of town is all about fun.

1 Medborgarplatsen

At the edges of the vast open square that is Medborgarplatsen, all the bars in the area have roped-off outdoor seating. The most relaxed among them is probably **Debaser Medis** (📞08-694 79 00; www.debaser.se; Medborgarplatsen 8; ⏱7pm-1am Sun-Thu, 8pm-3am Fri & Sat; Ⓜ Medborgarplatsen), but we recommend choosing a spot at whichever place offers the best eye candy.

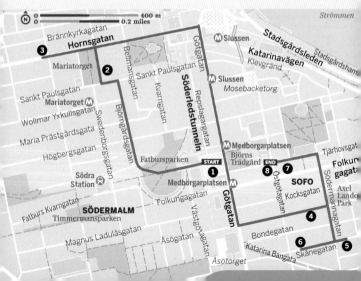

2 Mariatorget

Trek slightly northwest toward the lovely square Mariatorget, where you can enjoy a drink on the terrace or balcony of the ABBA-owned hotel **Rival** (☏08-54 57 89 24; www.rival.se; Mariatorget 3; ⊙5pm-midnight Thu-Sat; Ⓜ Mariatorget).

3 Marie Laveau

In an old sausage factory along Hornsgatan, **Marie Laveau** (www.marielaveau.se; Hornsgatan 66; ⊙11am-3am; Ⓜ Mariatorget) is a kicking Söder playpen that draws a boho-chic crowd. The designer-grunge bar (think chequered floor and subway-style tiled columns) serves killer cocktails, while the sweaty basement hosts club nights on the weekend. Known for its monthly 'Bangers & Mash' Britpop night – check online for a schedule.

4 Nada

Loop back toward the action: SoFo, south of Folkungagatan. With its soft orange glow, mini-chandelier and decadent black-toned back bar, **Nada** (☏08-644 70 20; Åsögatan 140; ⊙5pm-1am Mon-Sat; Ⓜ Medborgarplatsen) is a cosy establishment that pulls Söder's 20-/30-something party people. DJs play everything from alternative pop to '80s retro, while behind the bar mixologists sling elaborate summery cocktails.

5 Snotty's

A few blocks away from Nada, **Snotty's** (Skånegatan 90; pints around Skr52; ⊙4pm-1am) is a mellow hang-out, friendly and free of attitude. It's one of the most comfortable and unpretentious places to drink in Stockholm. It has a vaguely retro vibe, a smooth wooden bar and record covers all over the walls.

6 Bara Enkelt

Just down the street from Snotty's, decked out in shagalicious floral wallpaper and plush red sofas, **Bara Enkelt** (☏08-669 58 55; www.baras.se; Skånegatan 59; ⊙5pm-1am Mon-Sat; Ⓜ Medborgarplatsen), formerly Bara Vi, is a popular hang-out for trendy 30-somethings who like their drinks list long and smooth. Check online for a schedule of indie rock acts on stage.

7 Kebab Stop

Do as the locals do and stop for a greasy kebab at one of the carts on and around Medborgarplatsen – you'll need something to soak up all that adventure. For a sit-down version, try the friendly **Folkets Kebab** (Folkungagatan 63).

8 On the Corner

Wrap up the tour with a last stop at one of the very few places you can find a cheap beer in the city: the little collection of dive bars at the corner of Tjärhovsgatan and Östgötagatan. What they lack in ambience they make up for in affordability, and you're bound to meet a lively crowd here.

E   **F**   **G**   **H**

Strömmen

Ⓝ 0   200 m
0   0.1 miles

For reviews see
◉	Top Sights	p70
◉	Sights	p76
✕	Eating	p76
🍷	Drinking	p79
★	Entertainment	p80
🛍	Shopping	p81

bergsplan   **Slussen**

✕2   **Slussen**
1 Ⓜ
ckholms
dsmuseum   *Södermalmstorg*
rväders gränd   ●7
Ⓜ Slussen   **Katarinavägen**   Klevgränd   Stadsgårdshamnen   ◉ **Fotografiska**
18

Mosebacketorg   **Stadsgårdsleden**
✕10   Måster Mikaels   ✕4   **Stadsgårdsleden**
Högbergsgatan   Gata   Fjällgatan   Stadsgårdshamnen

edborgarplatsen   Kapellgränd   Stigbergsgatan
Ⓜ   21🛍   Tjärhovsplan
Björns   **Renstiernas Gata**   Stigbergsparken
Trädgård   **Folkungagatan**
dborgarplatsen   Tjärhovsgatan
●15   Beckbrännarbacken
17 Ⓜ Medborgarplatsen   **SOFO**
Kocksgatan   Axel   Borgmästargatan   Bondegatan
✕8   Landquist   Klippgatan
Park   9
✕

11
5   ✕   Skånegatan
✕   ●13   *Nytorget*   2◉▶
3◉▶
Götgatan   *Greta Garbos Torg*   *Vita Bergen*

Söderledstunneln   Östgötagatan   Malmgårdsvägen
Blekingegatan   ✕6
hellgonagatan   Gotlandsgatan
Ⓜ **Skanstull**   Katarina Bangata
Bjurholmsplan   **Ringvägen**
20   Ölandsgatan   *Lilla Blecktornsparken*
★

Sights

Stockholms Stadsmuseum
MUSEUM

1 Map p74, E2

Evocative exhibits cover Stockholm's development from fortified port to modern metropolis via plague, fire and good old-fashioned scandal. The museum is housed in a late 17th-century palace designed by Nicodemus Tessin the Elder. Temporary exhibitions are fresh and eclectic, focused on the city's ever-changing shape and spirit. Admission gets you a card good for one year here and at Medeltidsmuseet (p30). Note that the museum is scheduled to close for renovations from January 2015 until late 2016. (City Museum; www.stadsmuseum.stockholm.se; Ryssgården, Slussen; adult/child Skr100/free; ⊙11am-5pm Tue-Sun, to 8pm Thu; ⚿; MSlussen)

Spårvägsmuseet
MUSEUM

2 Map p74, H4

In a former bus depot near the Viking Line terminal, Stockholm's charmingly old-school transport museum is an atmospheric spot to spend a rainy afternoon. An impressive collection of around 40 vehicles includes several very pretty antique horse-drawn carriages, vintage trams and buses, and a retro tunnelbana carriage (complete with original advertisements). Kids can play tunnelbana driver (there's video from the driver's seat). Displays about the construction of the tunnel-bana system starting in 1933 are pretty mind-blowing. (Transport Museum; ☎08-686 17 60; www.sparvagsmuseet.sl.se; Tegelviksgatan 22; adult/child Skr50/free; ⊙10am-5pm Mon-Fri, 11am-4pm Sat & Sun; ⚿2, 66 Spårvägsmuseet)

Leksaksmuseet
MUSEUM

3 Map p74, H4

Sharing an entrance with Spårvägsmuseet, the Toy Museum is packed with everything you probably ever wanted as a child (and may still be hankering for as an adult). If anybody in your family just happens to be crazy about model trains, model aeroplanes, toy soldiers, toy robots, Barbie dolls or stuffed animals, don't miss it. (Toy Museum; ☎08-641 61 00; www.leksaksmuseet.se; Tegelviksgatan 22; with Spårvägsmuseet ticket free; ⊙10am-5pm Mon-Fri, 11am-4pm Sat & Sun; ⚿2, 66 Spårvägsmuseet)

Eating

Hermans Trädgårdscafé
VEGETARIAN $$

4 Map p74, G2

This justifiably popular vegetarian buffet is one of the nicest places to dine in Stockholm, with a glassed-in porch and outdoor seating on a terrace overlooking the city's glittering skyline. Fill up on inventive, flavourful veggie and vegan creations served from a cosy, vaulted room – you might need to muscle your way in, but it's

Spårvägsmuseet

worth the effort. (☑08-643 94 80; www.
hermans.se; Fjällgatan 23A; buffet Skr175,
desserts from Skr35; ☺11am-9pm; ✐; ☐2,
3, 53, 71, 76 Tjärhovsplan, ⓂSlussen)

Chutney VEGETARIAN $

5 Map p74, F4

Sitting among a string of three inviting cafes along this block, Chutney is
one of Stockholm's many well-
established vegetarian restaurants,
offering excellent value and great
atmosphere. The daily lunch special
is usually a deliciously spiced,
curry-esque heap of veggies over rice,
and includes salad, bread, coffee and
a second helping if you can manage it. (☑08-640 30 10; www.chutney.se;

Katarina Bangata 19; dagens lunch Skr80;
☺11am-10pm Mon-Sat, noon-9pm Sun; ✐;
ⓂMedborgarplatsen)

Pelikan SWEDISH $$

6 Map p74, F5

Lofty ceilings, wood panelling and
no-nonsense waiters in waistcoats
set the scene for classic *husmanskost*
at this century-old beer hall. The
herring options are particularly good
(try the 'SOS' plate, an assortment of
pickled herring; Skr124 to Skr138) and
there's usually a vegetarian special to
boot. There's a hefty list of aquavit,
too. (☑08-55 60 90 90; www.pelikan.
se; Blekingegatan 40; mains Skr172-285;
☺5pm-midnight or 1am; ⓂSkanstull)

Eriks Gondolen
SWEDISH $$$

7 🍴 Map p74, E2

Perched above Slussen atop the antique lift Katarinahissen, this place is known for top-notch Swedish food, refined service, perfect cocktails and endless views. There's a formal dining room (reservations recommended), or you can keep it a little more casual in the bar alone. In summer there's seating outdoors. (📞08-641 70 90; www.eriks.se; Stadsgården 6; mains Skr215-340; ⏰11.30am-11pm Mon, 11.30am-1am Tue-Fri, 4pm-1am Sat; Ⓜ Slussen)

Östgöta Källaren
SWEDISH $$

8 🍴 Map p74, F4

The regulars at this soulful pub-restaurant range from multipierced rockers to blue-rinse grandmas, all smitten with the dimly lit romantic atmosphere, amiable vibe and hearty Swedish, Eastern European and French-Mediterranean grub. Try the saffron shellfish casserole (Skr198).

Top Tip

Travelling with Children

Sweden is a fantastically fun and easy place to travel with children, from infants up to teens. Most sights and activities are designed with kids in mind, with free or reduced admission for under-18s and plenty of hands-on exhibits. Restaurants, accommodation and transport are also well accustomed to handling families.

(📞08-643 22 40; Östgötagatan 41; mains Skr155-225; ⏰5pm-1am Mon-Fri, 3pm-1am Sat, 5pm-1am Sun; Ⓜ Medborgarplatsen)

String
CAFE $

9 🍴 Map p74, G4

This retro-funky SoFo cafe does a bargain weekend brunch buffet (Skr80; 10.30am to 1pm Saturday and Sunday). Load your plate with everything from cereals, yoghurt and fresh fruit to pancakes, toast and amazing homemade hummus. Fancy that '70s chair you're plonked on? Take it home; almost everything you see is for sale. (📞08-714 85 14; www.cafestring.com; Nytorgsgatan 38; sandwiches Skr50-65, salads Skr80; ⏰9am-8pm Mon-Thu, to 7pm Fri, 10am-7pm Sat & Sun; Ⓜ Medborgarplatsen)

Crêperie Fyra Knop
CAFE $

10 🍴 Map p74, E2

Head here for perfect crêpes in an intimate setting, plus a hint of shanty-town chic – think reggae tunes and old tin billboards for Stella Artois. A good place for a quiet tête-à-tête before you hit the clubs down the street. (📞08-640 77 27; Svartensgatan 4; crêpes Skr64-84, galettes Skr100-118; ⏰5-11pm Mon-Fri, noon-11pm Sat & Sun; Ⓜ Slussen)

Koh Phangan
THAI $$

11 🍴 Map p74, F4

Best at night, this outrageously kitsch Thai restaurant has to be seen to be believed. Tuck into your *kao pat gai* (chicken fried rice) in a real *tuk-tuk* to the accompanying racket of crickets

Eriks Gondolen

and tropical thunder, or kick back with beers in a bamboo hut. DJs occasionally hit the decks and it's best to book ahead. (☑08-642 50 40; www.kohphangan. se; Skånegatan 57; starters Skr85-95, mains Skr155-285; ⊙4pm-1am Mon-Fri, noon-1am Sat & Sun; Ⓜ Medborgarplatsen)

Nystekt Strömming   SWEDISH $

 12 Map p74, E1

For a quick snack of freshly fried herring, seek out this humble cart outside the tunnelbana station at Slussen. Large or small combo plates come with big slabs of the fish and a selection of sides and condiments, from mashed potato and red onion to salads and hardbread; more portable

wraps and the delicious herring burger go for Skr55. (Södermalmstorg; combo plates Skr35-75; ⊙11am-8pm Mon-Fri, to 6pm Sat & Sun, closing times vary; Ⓜ Slussen)

Drinking

Pet Sounds Bar   BAR

13 Map p74, F4

A SoFo favourite, this jamming bar pulls in music journos, indie culture vultures and the odd goth rocker. While the restaurant serves decent Italian-French grub, the real fun happens in the basement. Head down for a mixed bag of live bands, release parties and DJ sets. Hit happy hour (2pm to 6pm) for drink specials. (www.

petsoundsbar.se; Skånegatan 80; beer Skr72, cocktails Skr118; M Medborgarplatsen)

Akkurat
BAR

14 Map p74, D2

Valhalla for beer fiends, Akkurat boasts a huge selection of Belgian ales as well as a good range of Swedish-made microbrews, including Nynäshamn's Ångbryggeri. It's one of only two places in Sweden to be recognised by a Cask Marque for its real ale. Extras include a vast wall of whisky, and mussels (half/full order Skr155/215) on the menu. (☑08-644 00 15; www.akkurat.se; Hornsgatan 18; beers Skr59-95; ☺11am-1am Mon-Fri, 3pm-1am Sat, 6pm-1am Sun; M Slussen)

Kvarnen
BAR

15 Map p74, E3

An old-school Hammarby football fan hang-out, Kvarnen is one of the best bars in Söder. The gorgeous beer hall dates from 1907 and seeps tradition; if you're not the clubbing type, get here early for a nice pint and a meal (mains Skr139 to Skr195). As the night progresses, the nightclub vibe takes over. Queues are fairly constant but justifiable. (☑08-643 03 80; www.kvarnen. com; Tjärhovsgatan 4; ☺11am-1am Mon-Tue, 11am-3am Wed-Fri, 5pm-3am Sat, 5pm-1am Sun; M Medborgarplatsen)

Vampire Lounge
BAR

The name says it all: this dark basement bar is bloodsucker-themed all the way through. There are perspex 'windows' in the floor showing buried caches of anti-vamp supplies such as holy water, crosses and garlic – just in case. Locals recommend the ice-cream cocktails. The lounge shares an entrance with Östgöta Källaren (see 8 Map p74, F4) restaurant. (www.vampirelounge.se; Östgötagatan 41; ☺5pm-1am Mon-Fri, 7pm-1am Sat; M Medborgarplatsen)

Lady Patricia
BAR

16 Map p74, B1

Half-price seafood, nonstop *schlager* music and decks packed with sexy Swedes and drag queens make this former royal yacht a gay Sunday night ritual (though you can now visit five nights a week). Head to the upper dance floor where lager-happy punters sing along to Swedish Eurovision entries with a bemusing lack of irony. (☑08-743 05 70; www.patricia.st; Söder Mälarstrand, Kajplats 19; ☺5pm-midnight Wed & Thu, to 5am Fri-Sun)

Entertainment

Debaser
LIVE MUSIC

17 Map p74, E3

This mini-empire of entertainment has its flagship rock venue (Debaser Medis; p72) on Medborgarplatsen. Emerging or bigger-name acts play most nights, while the killer club nights span anything from rock-steady to punk and electronica. (There are also a couple of restaurants around town and a location in Malmö.)

(☎08-694 79 00; www.debaser.se; Medborgarplatsen 8; ⊙7pm-1am Sun-Thu, 8pm-3am Fri & Sat; Ⓜ Medborgarplatsen)

Mosebacke Etablissement
LIVE MUSIC

18 ⭐ Map p74, E2

Eclectic theatre and club nights aside, this historic culture palace hosts a mixed line-up of live music. Tunes span anything from home-grown pop to antipodean rock. The outdoor terrace combines dazzling city views with a thumping summertime bar. (www.mosebacke.se; Mosebacketorg 3; tickets Skr80-400; ⊙6pm-late; Ⓜ Slussen)

Folkoperan
THEATRE

19 ⭐ Map p74, B2

Folkoperan gives opera a thoroughly modern overhaul with its intimate, cutting-edge and sometimes controversial productions. The under-26s enjoy half-price tickets. (☎08-616 07 50; www.folkoperan.se; Hornsgatan 72; tickets Skr145-455; Ⓜ Zinkensdamm)

Globen
LIVE MUSIC

20 ⭐ Map p74, E5

This huge white spherical building just south of Södermalm hosts regular big-name pop and rock concerts, as well as sporting events and trade fairs. Even if nothing's going on inside, you can take a ride up and over the building inside SkyView, a mini-globe whose glass walls offer great views across town. (☎077-131 0000; www.globen.se; Arenavägen; Ⓜ Globen)

Shopping

Chokladfabriken
CHOCOLATE

21 🅰 Map p74, G3

For an edible souvenir, head to this chocolate shop, where seasonal Nordic ingredients are used to make heavenly treats. In addition to chocolate boxes and hot-cocoa mix in gift boxes, there's a cafe for an on-the-spot fix, tastings, and a stash of speciality ingredients and utensils. (www.chokladfabriken.com; Renstiernas Gata 12; ⊙10am-6.30pm Mon-Fri, 10am-5pm Sat; Ⓜ Medborgarplatsen, Slussen)

Papercut
BOOKS

22 🅰 Map p74, B2

This shop sells books, magazines and DVDs with a high-end pop-culture focus. Pick up a new Field Notes journal and a decadent film journal or a gorgeous volume devoted to one of the many elements of style. (☎08-13 35 74; www.papercutshop.se; Krukmakargatan 24; ⊙11am-6.30pm Mon-Fri, 11am-5pm Sat, noon-4pm Sun; Ⓜ Zinkensdamm)

Explore

Östermalm

Östermalm is indisputably Stockholm's party district, where the beautiful, rich and famous come to play. It's also home to some of the city's best places to eat, drink and shop. But it isn't strictly about hedonism: this is also where you'll find two of the best museums about the country's battle-ridden past.

The Sights in a Day

☀️ Start your day with a visit to the engrossing **Historiska Museet** (p84), where you'll come face to face with episodes from Sweden's exciting history – and prehistory. It's a good-sized museum, so allow a couple of hours to really explore the place.

☀️ Take a break for lunch at the equally enthralling **Östermalms Saluhall** (p91), a gourmet food hall in a historic building. From fresh produce, fish and meat to imported cheese and exotic pastries, the market stalls sell just about everything. In between the counters are a number of excellent cafes where you can grab a bite.

🌙 After lunch, visit the sobering **Armémuseum** (p90) for a lesson in war history. Walk it off with some window-shopping and a latte at Sturekatten. Stop in for a decadent seafood dinner at **Sturehof** (p91), then glamorous drinks in a Stureplan bar like **Laroy** (p92).

For a local's day in Östermalm, see p86.

 Top Sights

Historiska Museet (p84)

 Local Life

Opulent Östermalm (p86)

❤️ **Best of Stockholm**

Eating
Lisa Elmqvist (p90)

Nightlife
Lilla Baren at Riche (p92)

Sturecompagniet (p92)

Spy Bar (p92)

Coffee Shops
Sturekatten (p91)

Café Saturnus (p91)

Getting There

Ⓜ️ **Tunnelbana** Östermalmstorg or Kungsträdgården to reach Östermalm

🚊 **Tram** 7, Nybroplan

Top Sights
Historiska Museet

The national historical collection awaits at this enthralling museum, which opened in 1943. From Iron Age skates and a Viking boat to medieval textiles and Renaissance triptychs, it spans over 10,000 years of Swedish history and culture. There's an exhibit about the medieval Battle of Gotland (1361), an excellent multimedia display on the Vikings, a room of altarpieces from the Middle Ages, a vast textile collection, and a section on prehistoric culture in what would become Scandinavia.

◉ Map p18; H4

www.historiska.se

Narvavägen 13-17

adult/child Skr100/free

⊘10am-6pm, closed Mon Sep-May

🚌44, 56, Ⓜ Karlaplan, Östermalmstorg

HISTORISKA MUSEET

Don't Miss

Gold Room

An undisputed highlight of the museum is the subterranean Gold Room, a dimly lit chamber gleaming with Viking plunder and other treasures, including the jewel-encrusted Reliquary of St Elisabeth (who died at 24 and was canonised in 1235). The most astonishing artefacts are the three 5th-century gold collars discovered in Västergötland in the 19th century. The largest consists of seven rings, weighs 823g and is decorated with 458 symbolic figures.

Tapestries

The museum is known for its large collection of medieval textiles, including several that would have been displayed in very early wooden churches in northern Swedish villages.

Vikings

The museum's impressive Viking-era exhibition attempts to correct popular misconceptions about the Vikings and their age, focusing on their work as traders and on the lives of ordinary folk in those days (which, it turns out, was not all longboats and pillaging – most people were farmers). It's also a good place to learn about the rune stones that are still found scattered randomly across Sweden.

Battle of Gotland

A new permanent exhibit brings to life the medieval Battle of Gotland, which in 1361 pitted the island's farmers against professional soldiers in the Danish army. Needless to say it did not go well for the farmers: some 1800 were thrown into mass graves outside Visby. Archaeological studies have led to a clearer picture of what happened, and the display, though gruesome, is fascinating.

☑ Top Tips

▶ The galleries are divided according to era: the upper floor holds the Middle Ages and baroque, the main (ground) floor is dedicated to prehistory, and the Gold Room is downstairs, with treasures from prehistory to medieval times.

▶ Captions in English describe the treasures and displays, and offer insights into each item's history and how it was made.

✗ Take a Break

There's a coffee shop and cafe near the entrance of the museum. For something more substantial, head up Linnégatan for Thai food in a vivid setting at Sabai-Soong (p92).

Local Life
Opulent Östermalm

Östermalm has come quite a long way from its early days as a cattle field. Now one of the wealthiest areas of Stockholm, its elegant buildings, lush parks and classy shops make it a dream to wander through. The addresses in this part of town may be exclusive, but its beauty is here for everyone to enjoy.

❶ Kungliga Biblioteket
Sweden's national library, Kungliga Biblioteket is beautifully situated in **Humlegården**, a leafy green park that acts as a neighbourhood oasis. The library holds a copy of virtually everything printed in Sweden or Swedish since 1661 (though it also has several much older items, including the 13th-century 'Devil's Bible'). You can visit or simply admire it as you wander the park.

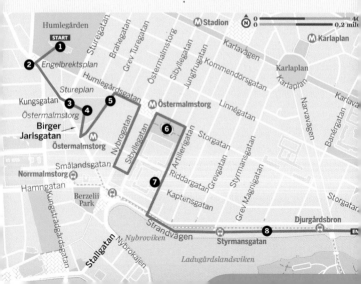

2 Vassa Eggen

If you've started your day in the local fashion – that is, none too early – it's probably getting close to lunchtime. Treat yourself to the surprisingly affordable weekday lunch (Skr145) at steakhouse **Vassa Eggen** (♪08-21 61 69; www.vassaeggen.com; Birger Jarlsgatan 29; ⊙11.30am-2pm Mon-Fri, 5.30-10pm Mon, to 11pm Tue-Sat; MÖstermalmstorg), a long-standing neighbourhood favourite with a domed dining room, floor-to-ceiling murals and edgy bar.

3 Svampen

Built in 1937, then smashed and rebuilt in the '80s, this oddball structure – originally meant to be rain protection – has become a landmark and one of the most popular places to meet people before heading out on the town. (*Svampen* means 'the Mushroom', by the way.)

4 Sturegallerian

Home to dozens of high-end boutiques as well as the exclusive and historic spa **Sturebadet** (♪08-54 50 15 00; www. sturebadet.se; Sturegallerian 36, Stureplan; day pass Skr495-595; ⊙6.30am-10pm Mon-Fri, 9am-7pm Sat & Sun; MÖstermalmstorg), this is not your average shopping mall, with interiors built to blend with the 19th-century facade.

5 Grev Turegatan

This pedestrianised shopping and dining street, along with Nybrogatan which runs parallel to the east, forms the core of the district – at any rate, the two streets offer a highly concen-

trated dose of what Östermalm does best, with one-of-a-kind retail shops and sophisticated eateries set among beautiful apartment buildings with elaborately decorated exteriors.

6 Hedvig Eleonora Kyrka

This pretty, octagonal church, consecrated in 1737, was initially designed by Jean de la Vallée in the 1660s and built as a private church for the Swedish Navy. The impressive pulpit was designed by Jean Eric Rehn, and the organ still has its original 1762 facade, by Carl Fredrik Aldencrantz. Frequent musical performances are held here – check the bulletin boards.

7 Kungliga Hovstallet

The Royal Stables occupy an enormous red-brick building that extends for most of a block. It was completed in 1894 and is a National Heritage building. The stables are part museum, part workplace – all royal-family transportation is arranged here, and the building holds 18 of the king's horses, as well as antique carriages and the royal car collection.

8 Strandvägen

Probably the fanciest address in the city, this boulevard is also one of the most pleasant to walk along, and it provides a stunning view across the water at the city skyline. Lined with proud houses sporting fairy-tale turrets, the street is nearly 80m wide, with a row of trees down the centre, making for quiet strolling.

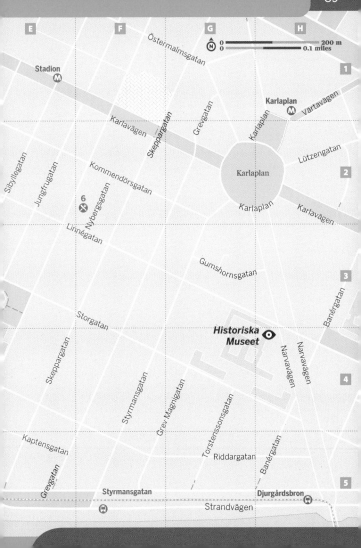

E

F

G

H

N 0   200 m
0   0.1 miles

Östermalmsgatan

Stadion Ⓜ

Karlaplan Ⓜ Värtavägen

Karlavägen

Grevgatan

Skeppargatan

Karlaplan

Lützengatan

1

Sibyllegatan

Jungfrugatan

Kommendörsgatan

Nybergsgatan

6 ✕

Karlaplan

Karlaplan Karlavägen

2

Linnégatan

Gumshornsgatan

Banérgatan

3

Storgatan

Historiska Museet ⊙

Narvavägen

Skeppargatan

Styrmansgatan

Grev Magnigatan

Torstenssonsgatan

Narvavägen

4

Kaptensgatan

Riddargatan

Banérgatan

Grevgatan

Styrmansgatan

Djurgårdsbron

Strandvägen

5

Sights

Armémuseum
MUSEUM

1 ⊙ Map p88, D3

Delve into the darker side of human nature at Armémuseum, where three levels of engrossing exhibitions explore the horrors of war through art, weaponry and life-size reconstructions of charging horsemen, forlorn barracks and starving civilians. You can even hop on a replica sawhorse for a taste of medieval torture. (Artillery Museum; ☑08-51 95 63 00; www.armemuseum.se; Riddargatan 13; adult/child Skr80/free; ⊙10am-7pm Jun-Aug, 11am-8pm Tue, to 5pm Wed-Sun Sep-May; ⓂÖstermalmstorg)

Eating

Lisa Elmqvist
SEAFOOD $$

Seafood fans, look no further. This Stockholm legend, suitably snug inside historic Östermalms Saluhall (see 2 ✖ Map p88, D3), is never short of a satisfied lunchtime crowd. The menu changes daily, so let the waitstaff order for you; whether it's lobster pancakes or seared Sichuan pepper char fillets, you won't be disappointed. Classics include shrimp sandwiches (Skr170) and a gravlax plate (Skr185). (☑08-55 34 04 10; www.lisaelmqvist.se; Östermalmstorg, Östermalms Saluhall; mains from Skr170; ⊙9.30am-6pm Mon-Thu, to 6.30pm Fri, to 4pm Sat; ⓂÖstermalmstorg)

Understand

It's the Water

- -

You'll see signs in many of Stockholm's hotels boasting that the city's tap water is among the cleanest on earth and perfectly good to drink. This is no exaggeration. There's virtually no excuse for buying bottled water in Sweden. Stockholm's tap water comes from Lake Mälaren in the middle of the city, itself clean enough that locals swim in it all summer and fish from it year-round.

Such close ties to the water may help explain Stockholmers' early and thorough embrace of 'green' environmental practices: when people walk past their water source every day on their way to work, it's difficult to ignore the importance of keeping it pure.

Water quality in and around the city is monitored by the Swedish National Food Administration; to learn more, visit www.stockholmvatten.se. Meanwhile, carry your own refillable water bottle and don't hesitate to fill it up right from the tap.

Östermalms Saluhall   MARKET $

 2 Map p88, D3

Stockholm's historic gourmet food market feeds all the senses with fresh fish, seafood and meat, fruit, vegetables and hard-to-find cheeses, as well as cafes for a quick lunch or snack. The 1885 building, a Stockholm landmark, is showing its age and will be closed for renovations from 2015 to 2017, with a temporary market set up in the square. (www.ostermalmshallen.se; Östermalmstorg; mains from Skr85; ⏱9.30am-6pm Mon-Thu, to 7pm Fri, to 4pm Sat; MÖstermalmstorg)

Sturehof   SEAFOOD $$$

3 Map p88, B3

Superb for late-night sipping and supping, this convivial brasserie sparkles with gracious staff, celebrity regulars and fabulous seafood-centric dishes (the bouillabaisse is brilliant). Both the front and back bars are a hit with the eye-candy brigade and perfect for a post-meal flirt. (☎08-440 57 30; www.sturehof.com; Stureplan 2; starters Skr155-265, mains Skr185-495; ⏱11am-2am Mon-Fri, noon-2am Sat & Sun; MÖstermalmstorg)

Café Saturnus   CAFE $

4 Map p88, A1

For velvety caffè latte, Gallic-inspired baguettes and perfect pastries, saunter into this casually chic bakery-cafe. Sporting a stunning mosaic floor, silky striped wallpaper and a few outdoor tables, it's a fabulous spot to flick

through the paper while tackling what has to be Stockholm's most enormous sweet roll (cinnamon or cardamom, take your pick). (☎08-611 77 00; Eriksbergsgatan 6; sweet rolls Skr50, salads & sandwiches Skr68-138; ⏱8am-8pm Mon-Fri, 9am-8pm Sat & Sun; 🚌2 Eriksbergsgatan)

Sturekatten   CAFE $

5 Map p88, C3

Looking like a life-size doll's house, this vintage cafe is a fetching blend of antique chairs, oil paintings, ladies who lunch and waitstaff in black-and-white garb. Slip into a salon chair, pour some tea and nibble on a piece of apple pie or a *kanelbulle* (cinnamon bun). (☎08-611 16 12; www.sturekatten.se; Riddargatan 4; pastries from Skr35; ⏱9am-7pm Mon-Fri, 10am-6pm Sat, 11am-6pm Sun; MÖstermalmstorg)

Sabai-Soong

THAI $$

6 Map p88, F2

Super-kitsch Sabai-Soong is keeping it real despite the snooty address. A hit with families and fashionistas alike, its tropical-trash day-glo interior is the perfect place to chow down on simple and faithful versions of *tod man pla* (Thai fish cakes) and fiery green curry. (08-663 12 77; www.sabai. se; Linnégatan 39B; 4.30-10pm Mon, to 11pm Tue-Thu, to midnight Fri, 4pm-midnight Sat, 4-10pm Sun; MÖstermalmstorg)

Drinking

Lilla Baren at Riche

BAR

7 Map p88, C4

A darling of Östermalm's hip parade, this pretty, glassed-in bar mixes smooth bar staff, skilled DJs and a packed crowd of fashion-literate

Local Life
Classy Cocktails

Laroy (08-54 50 37 00; Birger Jarlsgatan 20; admission Skr100; 10pm-3am Wed, Fri & Sat; MÖstermalmstorg) is in the same tall, pointy building as Spy Bar and draws the young and the beautiful for self-conscious cocktail sessions with a packed-in crowd. Make sure you're dressed to the hilt before trying your luck at charming the catwalk-worthy clientele. Tip: contact the venue a few days ahead to get your name on the door.

media types; head in by 9pm to score a seat. (08-54 50 35 60; Birger Jarlsgatan 4; 5pm-2am Tue-Sat)

Sturecompagniet

CLUB

8 Map p88, B3

Swedish soap stars, flowing champagne and look-at-me attitude set a decadent scene at this glitzy, mirrored and becurtained hallway. Dress to impress and flaunt your wares to commercial house. Big-name guest DJs come through frequently. (08-54 50 76 00; www.sturecompagniet.se; Stureplan 4; admission Skr120; 10pm-3am Thu-Sat; MÖstermalmstorg)

Spy Bar

CLUB

9 Map p88, B2

No longer the super-hip star of the scene it once was, the Spy Bar (aka 'the Puke' because *spy* means vomit in Swedish) is still a landmark and fun to check out if you're making the Östermalm rounds. It covers three levels in a turn-of-the-century flat (spot the tile stoves). (Birger Jarlsgatan 20; admission from Skr160; 10pm-5am Wed-Sat; MÖstermalmstorg)

Entertainment

Dramaten

THEATRE

10 Map p88, C4

The Royal Theatre stages a range of plays in a sublime art-nouveau environment. You can also take a guided tour in English at 4pm most days (adult/child Skr30/60), bookable online. (Kungliga Dramatiska Teatern; ☏08-667 06 80; www.dramaten. se; Nybroplan; tickets Skr90-390; ♿; ⓂKungsträdgården)

Shopping

Svenskt Tenn
ARTS, HOMEWARES

11 🔒 Map p88, D5

As much a museum of design as an actual shop, this iconic store is home to the signature fabrics and furniture of Josef Frank and his contemporaries. Browsing here is a great way to get a quick handle on what people mean by 'classic Swedish design' – and it's owned by a foundation that contributes heavily to arts funding. (www.svenskttenn.se; Nybrogatan 15; ☺10am-6.30pm Mon-Fri, 10am-5pm Sat, noon-4pm Sun; ⓂKungsträdgården)

Svensk Slöjd
ARTS, HANDICRAFTS

12 🔒 Map p88, D3

If you like the traditional Swedish wooden horses but want one that looks a little unique (or maybe you'd prefer a traditional wooden chicken instead?), check out this shop. It's crammed with quirky hand-carved knick-knacks as well as luxurious woven textiles, handmade candles, ironwork, knitted clothing and other high-quality gifts. (Nybrogatan 23; ☺10am-6pm Mon-Fri, 11am-6pm Sat; ⓂÖstermalmstorg)

Local Life
Vintage Books

From vintage Astrid Lindgren books to dusty 19th-century travel guides, the 100,000-strong collection of books here, many in English, make **Rönnells Antikvariat** (☏08-54 50 15 60; www.ronnells.se; Birger Jarlsgatan 32; ☺10am-6pm Mon-Fri, 11am-3pm Sat; ⓂÖstermalmstorg) one of the meatiest secondhand bookshops in town. Forage through the sales rack for a new dog-eared friend.

Nordiska Galleriet
ARTS, CRAFTS

13 🔒 Map p88, D3

This sprawling showroom is a design freak's El Dorado – think Hannes Wettstein chairs, Hella Jongerius sofas, Alvar Aalto vases and mini-sized Verner Panton chairs for style-sensitive kids. Luggage-friendly options include designer coathangers, glossy architecture books and bright Marimekko paper napkins. (www.nordiskagalleriet.se; Nybrogatan 11; ☺10am-6pm Mon-Fri, 10am-5pm Sat, noon-4pm Sun; ⓂÖstermalmstorg)

Hedengrens
BOOKS

14 🔒 Map p88, B3

Inside the upmarket Östermalm shopping mall is this great bookstore, with a huge selection of new fiction and nonfiction books in English. (☏08-611 51 32; Sturegallerian Shopping Centre; ☺10am-7pm Mon-Fri, 10am-5pm Sat, noon-5pm Sun; ⓂÖstermalmstorg)

Local Life
Museums of Gärdet & Ladugårdsgärdet

Getting There

Ⓜ Gärdet, then bus 1 or 76 to Frihamnen for Magasin 3

🚌 from Kaknästornet take bus 69

These two conjoined parklike areas – one a casual suburban neighbourhood, the other a former royal playground that's now a wide-open greenspace – contain some of the best museums in the city. And they're much easier to reach than they may initially seem – a quick bus or tunnelbana trip, or a leisurely walk from Östermalm.

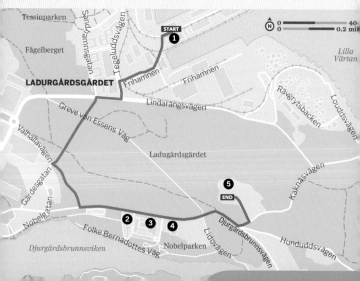

❶ Magasin 3

Though it's a bit out of the way and hours are limited, **Magasin 3** (☎08-54 56 80 40; www.magasin3.com; Elevator 4, Magasin 3 Bldg, Frihamnen; adult/child Skr40/free; ⏱11am-7pm Thu, to 5pm Fri-Sun, closed Jun-Aug & Christmas holidays; 🚊1, 76, Ⓜ Ropsten) is one of Stockholm's best contemporary-art galleries and well worth seeking out. Located in a dockside warehouse northwest of Kaknästornet, its six to eight annual shows often feature specially commissioned, site-specific work from the likes of Pipilotti Rist or American provocateur Paul McCarthy.

❷ Sjöhistoriska Museet

Across the large, open field of Ladugårdsgärdet from Magasin 3, you'll find a trio of excellent kid-friendly museums. The smallest and cutest of the three is this, the maritime museum – a must for fans of model ships (there are over 1500 mini vessels in the collection). The exhibits at **Sjöhistoriska Museet** (National Maritime Museum; Djurgårdsbrunnsvägen 24; admission free; ⏱10am-5pm Tue-Sun; 🚊69 Museiparken) also explore Swedish shipbuilding, sailors and life on deck.

❸ Tekniska Museet

Tekniska (Museum of Science & Technology; www.tekniskamuseet.se; Museivägen 7; adult/child Skr120/40, 5-8pm Wed free; ⏱10am-5pm Mon-Fri, 10am-8pm Wed, 11am-5pm Sat & Sun; 🚊69 Museiparken) is a sprawling wonderland of interactive science and technology exhibits

in the same complex. One of its biggest drawcards is **Cino4** (adult/child Skr80/40), Sweden's first '4D' multisensory cinema. The 'Teknorama' is a vast room of kinetic experiments and stations designed to do things like test your balance, flexibility and strength.

❹ Etnografiska Museet

Next door, the fascinating and atmospheric **Etnografiska Museet** (Museum of Ethnography; www.etnografiska.se; Djurgårdsbrunnsvägen 34; adult/child Skr80/free; ⏱11am-5pm Tue-Sun, to 8pm Wed; ♿; 🚊69 Museiparken) stages evocative displays on various aspects of non-European cultures, including dynamic temporary exhibitions and frequent live performances. Recent examples include a display about the cultural treasures of Afghanistan, Russian holiday traditions and 'real-life' voodoo.

❺ Kaknästornet

It's a nice walk to reach the big lookout tower that looms over this whole area. The 155m-tall **Kaknästornet** (www.kaknastornet.se; Mörka Kroken 28-30; adult/child Skr55/20; ⏱9am-10pm Mon-Sat, to 7pm Sun; 🚊69 Kaknästornet) is the automatic operations centre for radio and TV broadcasting in Sweden. Opened in 1967, it's among the tallest buildings in Scandinavia. There's an elevator up to the observation deck, restaurant and cafe near the top, from where there are stellar views of the city and archipelago. Plan on arriving near dusk on a clear day – sunsets from up here are amazing.

Top Sights
Millesgården

Getting There

Millesgården is on the island of Lidingö, northeast of the city.

Ⓜ Ropsten, then bus 207

Millesgården was from 1906 to 1931 the home and studio of sculptor Carl Milles (1875–1955), whose delicate water sprites and other whimsical sculptures dot the city landscape. The artist's delightful personality, which is clearly evident in his sculptures, also imbues the house where he lived and worked. It's a beautiful and inspiring place to visit, especially for anyone interested in art and design.

Sculpture park

Don't Miss

Art Gallery

The grounds include a crisp modern gallery in neoclassical style for changing exhibitions of contemporary art. Carl and Olga Milles themselves laid the tiles for the intricate black-and-white mosaic floor.

Sculpture Park

Milles transformed the rough hillside of the property into an exquisite outdoor sculpture garden, where items from ancient Greece, Rome, medieval times and the Renaissance intermingle with Milles' own creations. Seek out 'Little Austria', a garden space Milles designed for his wife to ease her homesickness. Most of the garden is arranged to evoke the Mediterranean coast.

Little Studio

Inside the sculpture park, the Little Studio, built by Milles' brother Evert, contains a fresco painting of the Bay of Naples. Black-and-white marble paths bordered by pines and birches, and crowned with Italianate columns, lead the way to the studio. The studio was initially built to improve the state of Milles' lungs, which suffered from the dust his work created.

Milles Home

The artist couple visited Pompeii in 1921, and after this trip they started adding elaborate Pompeiian touches to the decor – especially in what became the Red Room, with its mosaic floors and frescoed walls. Olga painted the kitchen cabinets after the Delft ceramic-tiled walls. The Music Room contains not only a grand piano but also a Donatello sculpture and a Canaletto painting, among other treasures.

☏ 08-446 75 90

www.millesgarden.se

Herserudsvägen 32

adult/child Skr100/free

⊙ 11am-5pm, closed Mon Oct-Apr

Ⓜ Ropsten, then bus 207

☑ Top Tips

▶ From mid-June through August, a 30-minute guided introduction in English is included in the ticket price, starting at 1.15pm Tuesday and Thursday.

✗ Take a Break

Millesgården Lanthandel (☏ 08-446 75 93; Herserudsvägen 28; lunch specials Skr120-175; ⊙ 11am-5pm, closed Mon Oct-Apr), a cafe and restaurant, occupies the middle terrace of the Sculpture Park. It serves coffee and cakes, lunch and dinner either outdoors on the terrace or inside by the fireplace in winter.

Explore

Kungsholmen

Until recently something of an underappreciated gem, especially among visitors, Kungsholmen is coming into its own. This is a laid-back mostly residential neighbourhood with great places to eat, kid-friendly parks and an amazingly long stretch of tree-lined water-side walking. Plus it's home to one of Stockholm's most important buildings, architecturally and practically, in Stadshuset (City Hall).

The Sights in a Day

☀ Start your day with a hearty breakfast at **Vurma** (p103), the warm-hearted and welcoming neighbourhood cafe that's a local favourite. Fuelled up, take a waterside stroll down to **Stadshuset** (p100) for a thorough tour – don't neglect to visit the tower.

☀ Spend the middle of the day wandering the area around Scheelegatan and Hantverkargatan (see p105) in search of an inspiring lunch destination. You'll have plenty to choose from – this is a great neighbourhood for ethnic eateries, so just opt for anything that strikes your fancy. Don't be surprised if you're also tempted to do some window-shopping.

☽ Afterward, walk off lunch along the water, following Norr Mälarstrand as far as you feel like going. Turn around and head back toward town, stopping for a leisurely drink and satisfying dinner at the exceptionally friendly and pretty floating restaurant **Mälarpaviljongen** (p103).

◉ **Top Sights**

Stadshuset (p100)

♥ **Best of Stockholm**

Architecture
Stadshuset (p100)

LGBT
Mälarpaviljongen (p103)

Free
Swimming at Stadshuset (p100)

Rålambshovsparken (p107)

Eating
Mälarpaviljongen (p103)

Vurma (p103)

Getting There

Ⓜ **Tunnelbana** Rådhuset, Fridhemsplan

Walk It's a short walk across Stadshusbron from the area around Centralstationen.

Top Sights
Stadshuset

The mighty Stadshuset (City Hall) dominates Stockholm's architecture, looking stern and weighty from far away but secretly aglitter inside. Built of about eight million bricks, it was designed by architect Ragnar Östberg, a proponent of the Swedish National Romantic style, and opened in 1923. Aside from serving as a striking landmark, it holds the offices of more than 200 government workers, as well as its better-known banquet halls and courtyards.

◉ Map p102; E4

www.stockholm.se/stadshuset

Hantverkargatan 1

adult/child Skr100/free

🕑9.30am-4pm, admission by tour only

🚊3, 62 Stadshuset,
Ⓜ Rådhuset

Don't Miss

The Tower

Atop the building's 106m-high tower is a golden spire featuring the heraldic symbol of Swedish power: the three royal crowns. Entry is by guided tour only; tours in English take place every 30 to 40 minutes between 9.30am and 4pm in summer, less frequently the rest of the year. There are stellar views and it's a great thigh workout.

Golden Hall

Nestled in the centre of Stadshuset is the glittering, mosaic-lined Gyllene salen (Golden Hall). The beguiling mosaics, made from 19 million bits of gold leaf, are by Einar Forseth (1892–1988). The post-Nobel banquet dancing and festivities happen here.

Prins Eugen's Fresco

Prins Eugen, who became a successful artist and was a generous patron of the arts, donated his own fresco painting of the lake view from the gallery, *The City on the Water*, which can be seen along one wall in the Prince's Gallery. Along the other wall are windows opening on to an impressive real-life version of the city on the water.

Stadshusparken

Don't neglect the lovely park abreast of Stadshuset, pretty in all seasons, with its views of Riddarholmen across the water. Two statues by Carl Eldh guard the steps, and Christian Eriksson's *Engelbrekt the Freedom Fighter* graces a pillar in the corner of the park. If the weather's warm, do as Stockholmers do and take a swim or sunbathe on the concrete platform.

☑ Top Tips

▶ Note that the tower and tower museum are only open for visits from May through September.

▶ If you're not quite sure you're up for walking 106m worth of stairs, there's an elevator that will take you halfway to the top.

✕ Take a Break

You can dine like a Nobel Prize winner at the restaurant in the basement of Stadshuset, **Stadshuskällaren** (☏ 08-586 218 30; www.stadshuskallarensthlm.se; mains lunch/dinner from Skr125/185). The Nobel menu costs Skr1695 and comes with a souvenir numbered menu. (Larger groups can choose any year's menu they fancy.) Regular mains are mostly hearty traditional meat-and-veg courses. There's also a variety of multicourse menu options for both lunch and dinner. Reservations are recommended.

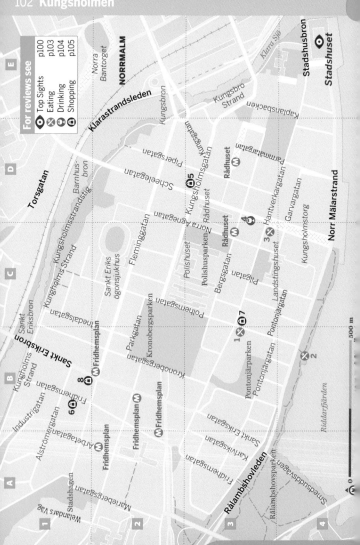

NORRMALM

Norra
Bantorget

Klarastrandsleden

Torsgatan

Kungsbron

Kungsbro
Strand

Kungsgatan

Klara Sjö

Stadshusbron

Stadshuset

Kaplansbacken

Barnhus-
bron

Kungsholmsstrandsstig

Piperstgatan

Scheelegatan

Kungsholmsgatan

❺

Rådhuset Ⓜ

Parmmätaregatan

Kungsholms Strand

Sankt
Eriksbron

Kungsholmsstrand

Sankt Eriks
ögonsjukhus

Fleminggatan

Norra Agnegatan

Rådhuset

Rådhuset Ⓜ

❹

Hantverkargatan

Garvargatan

❸

Kungsholmstorg

Norr Mälarstrand

Polishuset

Polishusparken

Bergsgatan

Pilgatan

Landstingshuset

Pontonjärgatan

Sankt Eriksplan

Fridhemsplan Ⓜ

Parkgatan

Kronobergsparken

Polhemsgatan

❶✖ ❼🛍

Pontonjärparken

Pontonjärgatan

Pontonjärgatan

Kungholms Strand

Industrigatan

Arbetargatan

Fridhemsplan Ⓜ

❽Ⓜ

❾🛍

Fridhemsplan

Fridhemsplan Ⓜ

Sankt Eriksgatan

Karlbergsvägen

Karlviksgatan

✖❷

Riddarfjärden

Alströmergatan

Welanders Väg

Stadshagen

Marieberssgatan

Fridhemsgatan

Rålambshovleden

Rålambshovsparken

Smedsuddsvägen

Smedsuddsvägen

500 m

E   D   C   B   A

1   2   3   4

Fish cake and salad

Eating

Vurma

CAFE **S**

1 ⊗ Map p102, B3

Squeeze in among the locals at this friendly cafe-bakery, a reliably affordable place to get a healthy and substantial meal in an unfussy setting. The scrumptious sandwiches and salads are inspired, with ingredients like halloumi, felafel, cured salmon, avocado and greens over quinoa or pasta. The homemade bread that comes with your order is divine. (www. vurma.se; Polhemsgatan 15-17; salads Skr108, sandwiches Skr60-80; ⊙7am-7pm Mon-Fri, 8am-7pm Sat & Sun; 🛜🗐🖈; Ⓜ Rådhuset)

Mälarpaviljongen

SWEDISH, AMERICAN **$$**

2 ⊗ Map p102, B4

When the sun's out, few places beat this alfresco waterside spot for some Nordic *dolce vita*. Its glassed-in gazebo, vast floating terrace and surrounding herb gardens are only upstaged by the lovely and supremely welcoming service. Both food and cocktails are beautified versions of the classics: huge burgers, pretty salmon salads, strawberry mojitos etc. Opening times are at the weather's mercy. (☎08-650 87 01; www.malarpaviljongen. se; Norr Mälarstrand 63; mains Skr168-235; ⊙11am-1am; Ⓜ Rådhuset)

Bergamott

FUSION $$$

3 Map p102, C3

The very cool French chefs in this kitchen don't simply whip up to-die-for French-Italian dishes, they'll probably deliver them to your table, talk you through the produce and guide you through the wine list. It's never short of a convivial crowd, so it's best to book, especially when jazz musicians drop in for a soulful evening jam. (08-650 30 34; www.

restaurangbergamott.se; Hantverkargatan 35; mains Skr195-325; 5.30pm-midnight Tue-Sat; Rådhuset)

Drinking

Lemon Bar

BAR

4 Map p102, D3

A favourite among locals for its laid-back vibe, the Lemon Bar epitomises the kind of comfy neighbour-

---

Understand
Swedish Must-Reads

One of the best ways to get inside the collective mind of a country is to read its top authors. Some of the most popular works by Swedish authors include *The Long Ships* (1954) by Frans Gunnar Bengtsson, *The Wonderful Adventures of Nils* (1906–07) by Selma Lagerlöf, the *Emigrants* series (1949–59) by Vilhelm Moberg, *Marking* (1963–64) by Dag Hammarskjöld, *Röda Rummet* (1879) by August Strindberg, *The Evil* (1981) by Jan Guillou and, more recently, *A Man Called Ove* (2013) by Fredrik Backman.

But it's Swedish crime fiction that has drawn the most attention recently. The massive success of the Millennium Trilogy, by the late journalist Stieg Larsson (he was the second-best-selling author in the world for 2008), has brought new and well-deserved attention to the genre, which was already thriving domestically. *The Girl with the Dragon Tattoo* (originally titled 'Men who Hate Women'; 2005) is the tip of the iceberg when it comes to this genre; Swedish crime writers have a long and robust history.

A few names to start with, if you're interested in exploring further, include Håkan Nesser, whose early novels *The Mind's Eye* (1993) and *Woman with Birthmark* (1996) have recently been translated into English, and Sweden's best-known crime fiction writer, Henning Mankell, whose novels are mostly set in Ystad and feature moody detective Kurt Wallander. Johan Theorin's quartet of mysteries (starting with *Echoes from the Dead*, 2008) is set on the island of Öland. Other writers to seek out include Karin Alvtegen (dubbed Sweden's 'queen of crime'), Kerstin Ekman, Camilla Läckberg and Jens Lapidus.

hood joint you can drop into on the spur of the moment and count on finding a friendly crowd and good music, mostly Swedish pop hits that may or may not result in dancing. (☎08-650 17 78; www.lemonlokal.se; Scheelegatan 8; cocktails Skr122; ⏱5pm-1am Tue-Sat; Ⓜ Rådhuset)

Shopping

Frank Form
CLOTHING

5 🔒 Map p102, D3

Fetching interior design, fashion and jewellery you're unlikely to find elsewhere in town, including pieces from the UK, Spain and the Czech Republic. Pick up slinky guys' sweaters from Basque label Loreak Mendian, a classic handbag from Irish designer Orla Kiely or one-off jewellery from Swedish designer Jezebel, commissioned specially for the store. (☎08-54 55 05 00; www.frankform.se; Kungsholmsgatan 20; ⏱11am-6.30pm Mon-Fri, to 4.30pm Sat; Ⓜ Rådhuset)

Grandpa
ACCESSORIES, CLOTHING

6 🔒 Map p102, B1

With a design inspired by the hotels of the French Riviera during the '70s, Grandpa's second Stockholm location is crammed with atmosphere, as well as artfully chosen vintage and faux-vintage clothing, cool and quirky accessories and whatnots, random hairdryers, suitcases and old radios,

plus a cool little cafe serving good espresso. (☎08-643 60 81; www.grandpa. se; Fridhemsgatan 43; ⏱11am-7pm Mon-Fri, to 5pm Sat, noon-4pm Sun; Ⓜ Fridhemsplan)

59 Vintage Store
CLOTHING

7 🔒 Map p102, C3

This rack-packed nirvana of retro threads will have you playing dress-up for hours. Both girls and boys can expect high-quality gear from the 1950s to the 1970s, including glam, mid-century ball-gowns, platform boots, Brit-pop blazers, *Dr Zhivago* faux-fur hats and the odd sequined sombrero. (☎08-652 37 27; www.59vintagestore.se; Hantverkargatan 59; ⏱noon-7pm Mon-Fri, noon-4pm Sat; Ⓜ Rådhuset)

 Local Life
Street Eats

There are plenty of interesting places to eat in Kungsholmen, but you'll find a particularly good and varied range of eateries along **Scheelegatan** and **Hantverkargatan** where the two streets intersect. Look for happy crowds spilling out of small ethnic restaurants and into sidewalk tables.

Once you're sated, move on to the nearby Lemon Bar for some well-crafted cocktails and good music.

Understand
Viking History

Scandinavia's greatest impact on world history probably occurred during the Viking Age, when hardy Norsemen set sail for other shores. The Swedish Vikings were more inclined towards trade than their Norwegian or Danish counterparts but their reputation as fearsome warriors was fully justified. At home it was the height of paganism; Viking leaders claimed descent from Freyr, 'God of the World', and celebrations at Uppsala involved human sacrifices.

In a Word
The word 'Viking' is derived from *vik*, meaning bay or cove, and is probably a reference to Vikings' anchorages during raids. You can still see the root word in many Swedish place names – Örnsköldsvik, in northern Sweden, for example, or Alvik, a suburban Stockholm tunnelbana stop.

Hit & Run Raids
The Vikings sailed a new type of boat that was fast and highly manoeuvrable, but sturdy enough for ocean crossings. Initial hit-and-run raids along the European coast were followed by major military expeditions, settlement and trade. The well-travelled Vikings settled part of the Slavic heartland, giving it the name 'Rus' and ventured as far as Newfoundland, Constantinople (modern-day Istanbul) and Baghdad, setting up trade with the Byzantine Empire.

Christianity Takes Hold
Christianity only took hold when Sweden's first Christian king, Olof Skötkonung (c 968–1020) was baptised. However, by 1160, King Erik Jedvarsson (Sweden's patron saint, St Erik) had virtually destroyed the last remnants of paganism.

Learn More About the Vikings
The Vikings, by Magnus Magnusson, is an extremely readable history book, covering their achievements in Scandinavia (including Sweden), as well as their wild deeds around the world. The historic Viking trading centre of Birka, on Björkö in Lake Mälaren, is an easy way to get an up-close look at Viking history; **Strömma Kanalbolaget** (www.stromma.se) runs round-trip cruises.

Smedsuddsbadet

Västermalmsgallerian

SHOPPING CENTRE

8 🔒 Map p102, B1

This busy mall is home to some note-worthy residents. Pick up Scandi-design at DesignTorget, sexy Swedish briefs at Björn Borg, cult cosmetics at Face Stockholm and demo-cratically priced kids' and women's threads at H&M. (📞08-737 20 00; www.vastermalmsgallerian.se; St Eriksgatan 45; ⏰10am-7pm Mon-Fri, to 5pm Sat, 11am-5pm Sun; Ⓜ Fridhemsplan)

◯ Local Life
Urban Beaches

Kungsholmen boasts the largest beach in the Stockholm city centre, called **Smedsuddsbadet**. At the first sign of warm weather in spring, locals flock here to soak up the sun after the long, dark Swedish winter. To find the beach, follow the foot-path along Norr Mälarstrand west beside the water toward **Rålamb-shovsparken** (Ⓜ Fridhemsplan). (You'll also see people sunbathing and swimming from the Stadshuset terrace.)

Top Sights
Drottningholm

Getting There

Drottningholm is 10km west of Stockholm.

⚓ Strömma Kanalbolaget boats depart frequently from Stadshusbron in Stockholm (one hour one-way; round trip Skr195).

The royal residence and parks of Drottningholm on Lovön are justifiably popular attractions and easy to visit from the capital. Home to the royal family for part of the year, Drottningholm's Renaissance-inspired main palace was designed by architectural great Nicodemus Tessin the Elder and begun in 1662, about the same time as Versailles.

Don't Miss

Hedvig Eleonora's Bedchamber
The highly ornamented State Bedchamber of Hedvig Eleonora (1636–1715), consort of King Karl X Gustav, is Sweden's most expensive baroque interior. It's decorated with paintings featuring the childhood of their son, who would become King Karl XI. The painted ceiling shows the queen consort with her king.

Karl X Gustav Gallery
The Karl X Gustav Gallery, in baroque style, depicts this monarch's militaristic exploits – though the paintings on the ceiling are of classical battle scenes, lending their mythical heft to Karl X's persona.

Library
Although the bulk of Queen Lovisa Ulrika's collection of 2000 books has been moved to the Royal Library in Stockholm for safekeeping, her library here is still a bright and impressive room, complete with most of its original 18th-century fittings.

Corps de Garde
The Lower North Corps de Garde was originally a guard room, bare and functional, but as the need for armed guards just outside the door diminished, this room was repurposed and beautified. It's now replete with gilt-leather wall hangings, which used to feature in many palace rooms during the 17th century.

Staircase
The palace's elaborate staircase, with statues and *trompe l'œil* embellishments at every turn, was the work of both of the Nicodemus Tessins, the Elder and the Younger. From the landing you can

---

☎ 08-402 62 80

www.kungahuset.se

adult/child Skr120/free, combined ticket incl Kina Slott Skr180/free

🕑 10am-4.30pm May-Aug, 11am-3.30pm rest of year, closed mid-Dec–Jan

Ⓜ Brommaplan, then bus 301-323 Drottningholm, 🚢 Stadshuskajen (summer only)

☑ Top Tips
▶ You can roam on your own, but it's worth taking a one-hour guided tour (Skr10; in English at 10am, noon, 2pm and 4pm June to August, noon and 2pm rest of year).

✕ Take a Break
Bring a picnic with you and enjoy lunch out in the gardens, or munch away at one of the restaurants by the palace. Drottningholms Paviljongen (p103) has a lovely terrace by the water outside the palace's main entrance.

gaze out at the gardens, of a similarly clever geometrical design angled to impress – filled with fountains and labyrinths, these are well worth exploring.

Drottningholms Slottsteater

Performances are held at Drottningholms Slottsteater in summer using 18th-century machinery, including ropes, pulleys, wagons and wind machines that allow scenes to be changed in less than seven seconds. Illusion was the order of the day,

and accordingly the theatre makes use of fake marble, fake curtains and papier-mâché viewing boxes.

Drottningholms Teatermuseum

The still-working Slottsteater, completed in 1766 on the instructions of Queen Lovisa Ulrika, is also a museum. Remarkably untouched until 1922, it's now the oldest theatre in the world still in its original state. The fascinating guided tour includes an Italianate room with fake 3D wall effects and a ceiling that looks like the sky.

Kina Slott

At the far end of the royal gardens is Kina Slott, a lavishly decorated Chinese pavilion built by King Adolf Fredrik as a birthday surprise for Queen Lovisa Ulrika in 1753. Restored between 1989 and 1996, it boasts one of the finest rococo chinoiserie interiors in Europe. Admission (Skr100) includes guided tours, which run at 11am, 1pm and 3pm daily from June to August (fewer in May and September).

Guards' Tent

On the slope below Kina Slott, the carnivalesque Guards' Tent was erected in 1781 as quarters for the dragoons of Gustav III, but it's not really a tent at all. The building now has displays about the gardens and Drottningholm's Royal Guard.

Understand
Hedvig Eleonora

The queen consort of King Karl X Gustav, Hedvig Eleonora was by all accounts a great beauty and a strong leader. After the king's death in 1660, she became regent until their son, Karl XI, came of age. When he died in 1697, she returned to that position, but only briefly, until her grandson, Karl XII, became king. Both son and grandson were devoted to Hedvig Eleonora and took her counsel seriously. Hers was an age of intrigue and gossip, rumoured affairs and various sordid alliances, both personal and political. She loved the theatre, had a gambling habit, and liked to party.

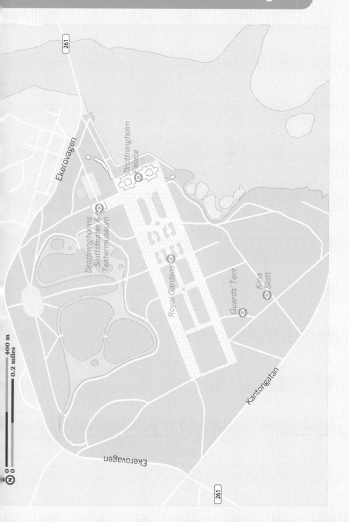

Ekerövägen

261

Drottningholm Palace

Drottningholms Slottsteater & Teatermuseum

Royal Gardens

Guards Tent

Kina Slott

Kantongatan

Ekerövägen

261

400 m

0.2 miles

Explore

Vasastan

This relaxed, residential neighbourhood has some of the best places to eat in Stockholm, along with several great hotels and two slick new art galleries in impressive buildings. It's also home to one of the greatest examples of Scandinavian architecture, Stadsbiblioteket. Wander around, take a nap in a park, and join the laid-back locals in just hanging out.

The Sights in a Day

☀ Why not start your day with a bit of Strindbergian drama? Pop in to **Strindbergsmuseet** (p115) inside the Blue Tower, the last home of the famously turbulent writer and painter. Afterward, revive your mood with a coffee and a gorgeous pastry at **Xoko** (p116). Then continue in the arts vein with a visit to **Sven-Harrys Konstmuseum** (p115), where edgy temporary exhibits complement the building's sleek design.

☀ Grab lunch at cosy and comfortable **Vurma** (p116). If you're not in a big rush, stop in for an afternoon pint at the old Swedish beer hall **Tennstopet** (p117). Continue walking up along Odengatan for a view of the elegant public library, **Stadsbiblioteket** (p115), designed by noted Swedish architect Erik Gunnar Asplund.

☾ Meander over toward the impressively housed **Bonniers Konsthall** (p115), designed by architect Johan Celsing and filled with enough shiny objects to occupy you until dinnertime. Your dining options in this neighbourhood are fantastic – if you're in the mood for upscale traditional Swedish cuisine with stellar presentation and top-notch service but an unfussy atmosphere, opt for **Tranan** (p116), a local favourite.

 Best of Stockholm

Museums & Galleries
Bonniers Konsthall (p115)

Architecture
Stadsbiblioteket (p115)

Eating
Lao Wai (p115)

Tranan (p116)

Vurma (p116)

Free
Stadsbiblioteket (p115)

Parks
Observatorielunden (p116)

Vasaparken (p116)

Getting There

Ⓜ **Tunnelbana** St Eriksplan, Odenplan, Rådmansgatan

NORRMALM

Birger Jarlsgatan

VASASTAN

200 m
0.1 miles

Vanadislunden

Roslagsgatan

Tulegatan

Sveavägen

Jarla-
parken

Eriksbergs-
parken

Rådmansg

Johannes
kyrka

Döbelnsgatan

Luntmakargatan

Kungstensgatan

Jarlaplan

Rehnsgatan

Markvardsgatan

Odengatan

Surbrunnsgatan

Spelbomskans
Torg

Stadsbiblioteket

Rådmansgatan

Saltmätargatan

Strindbergsmuseet

Hagagatan

Jurid-
icum

Observato-
rielunden

Drottninggatan

Teknologgatan

Tegnér-
lunden

Norrtullsgatan

Upplandsgatan

Odenplan

Vegagatan

Observatoriegatan

Dalagatan

Tegnérgatan

Enkehusparken

Västmannagatan

Freigatan

Odengatan

Sabbatsbergs
sjukhus

Vanadisvägen

Tre
Liljor

Idungatan

Änglingagatan

Sankt
Eriksparken

St Eriksgatan

Väster\åsgatan

Hudiksvallsgatan

Vanadisplan

Hälsinge-
höjden

Halsingegatan

Sigtunagatan

Vasaparken

Sven-Harrys
Konstmuseum

Bonniers
Konsthall

Kiarastr

Hälsingegatan

Vasaplan

Gästrikegatan

Tosplan

Torsplan

Gävlegatan

Solvändan

Torsgatan

Karlbergsvägen

Rödabergsg

Hälsingegatan

St Eriksplan

St Eriksplan

Birkagatan

Rörstrandsgatan

Sankt
Eriksplan

Atlasgatan

Atlasmuren

Sankt
Eriksbron

Kng

Norra
Stationsgatan

Norra Länken

Vikingagatan

Sights

Bonniers Konsthall

GALLERY

1 Map p114, B4

This ambitious gallery keeps culture fiends busy with a fresh dose of international contemporary art, as well as a reading room, a fab cafe and a busy schedule of art seminars and artists-in-conversation sessions. The massive, transparent flatiron building was designed by Johan Celsing. There are discussions about the exhibitions in English at 1pm, 3pm, 5pm and 7pm Wednesdays, and 1pm and 4pm Thursday to Sunday. Sunday at 2pm there are free guided tours by the museum's curators. (☑08-736 42 55; www. bonnierskonsthall.se; Torsgatan 19; adult/ child Skr80/free; ☉noon-8pm Wed, to 5pm Thu-Sun; Ⓜ St Eriksplan)

Stadsbiblioteket

LIBRARY

2 Map p114, D2

The main city library is just north of the city centre. Designed by architect Erik Gunnar Asplund and sporting a curvaceous, technicolour reading room, it's the finest example of Stockholm's 1920s neoclassicist style. (☑08-50 83 10 60; Sveavägen 73; admission free; ☉9am-7pm Mon-Fri, noon-4pm Sat; Ⓜ Odenplan)

Sven-Harrys Konstmuseum

MUSEUM

3 Map p114, B3

This slick new building houses an art gallery with interesting temporary exhibitions (recently a survey of Swedish fashion from 2000 to 2010), as well as a re-creation of the former Lidingö home of owner and art collector Sven-Harry Karlsson. Access to the home is by guided tour (Skr150, 40 minutes, currently in Swedish only). There's also an award-winning restaurant with terrace seating facing the park. (☑08-51 16 00 60; www.sven-harrys.se; Eastmansvägen 10-12; adult/child Skr100/free; ☉11am-7pm Wed-Fri, to 5pm Sat & Sun; Ⓜ Odenplan)

Strindbergsmuseet

MUSEUM

4 Map p114, D4

The small but evocative Strindbergsmuseet in the Blue Tower is the well-preserved apartment where writer and painter August Strindberg (1849–1912) spent his final four years. Peep into his closet, scan his study and library (containing some 3000 volumes), do a round of the dining room, and take in the often absorbing temporary exhibits. (☑08-411 53 54; www.strindbergsmuseet. se; Drottninggatan 85; adult/child Skr60/free; ☉10am-4pm Tue-Sun; Ⓜ Rådmansgatan)

Eating

Lao Wai

VEGETARIAN $$

5 Map p114, D3

Tiny, herbivorous Lao Wai does sinfully good things to tofu and vegetables, hence the faithful regulars. Everything here is gluten-free and vegan. A different lunch special is served each weekday; the dinner menu is more

Local Life

Park Life

Vasastan contains some of the most pleasant parks in Stockholm. On the hill behind Stadsbiblioteket is **Observatorielunden**, a park surrounding the historic Stockholm Observatory, now a part of Stockholm University. At its base, near the Rådmansgatan tunnelbana station, is a little skatepark, and fields where people sit reading or sunning; trails wind up and over the hill from here.

Not far away is **Vasaparken**, which abuts Sven-Harrys konstmuseum. It has a football pitch, another skatepark and a climbing wall, but most of it is simply park space with some shade trees, custom-designed for relaxing,

expansive, offering virtuous treats like Sichuan-style smoked tofu with shitake, chillies, garlic shoots, snow peas and black beans. (📞08-673 78 00; www.laowai. se; Luntmakargatan 74; dagens lunch Skr100, dinner mains Skr195-215; ⏰11am-2pm Mon-Fri, 5.30-9pm Tue-Sat; 🖊; Ⓜ Rådmansgatan)

Tranan

SWEDISH **$$$**

 6 Map p114, C2

Locals pack this former beer hall, now a comfy but classy neighbourhood bistro with a seafood-heavy menu and red-checked tablecloths. The food combines Swedish *husmanskost* with savvy Gallic touches; don't miss the fried herring. In summer, choose an outdoor

table and watch the human dramas across Odenplan. On the weekends, DJs and live bands perform in the basement bar. (📞08-52 72 81 00; www.tranan.se; Karlbergsvägen 14; starters Skr95-285, mains Skr195-345; ⏰5-11pm; Ⓜ Odenplan)

Vurma

CAFE **$$**

 7 Map p114, B3

Another branch of the popular cafe, this one near St Eriksplan, with great salads and sandwiches. (www.vurma.se; Gästrikegatan 2; salads Skr109; ⏰9am-7pm Mon-Sat, 10am-7pm Sun; 🖊; Ⓜ St Eriksplan)

Xoko

BAKERY **$**

8 Map p114, A3

Famous for making the desserts served at the Nobel Prize banquet, Xoko looks like a jewellery store, with row after row of gorgeous-looking edible gems on display. The cakes, sweets and truffles are crazy inventive, but you can also get outstanding versions of more humble and traditional fare – simple breads, sandwiches and cinnamon buns. Staff are entertaining and helpful. (📞08-31 84 87; www.xoko. se; Rörstrandsgatan 15; breakfast Skr59-95, pastries from Skr25; ⏰7am-7pm Mon-Fri, 8am-6pm Sat & Sun; Ⓜ St Eriksplan)

Caffè Nero

CAFE **$$**

 9 Map p114, E2

Packed with local hipsters during the busy lunch hour, this stylish but casual neighbourhood cafe serves substantial meals (fish, pasta, salads)

Xoko

at good prices, plus sublime coffee drinks and pastries. There's also a Saturday brunch from noon to 3pm. Next door is a sleek bar-restaurant, **Buco Nero**, open late with DJs and an upscale dinner menu (mains Skr195 to Skr295). (www.nerostockholm.se; Roslagsgatan 4; dagens lunch Skr100, mains Skr100-145; ☻7am-5pm Mon-Fri, 9am-5pm Sat & Sun; Ⓜ Odenplan, Rådmansgatan)

Tennstopet   SWEDISH, PUB FOOD $$

 Map p114, C3

Had there been a Swedish version of *Cheers*, it would've been filmed here. Oil paintings, gilded mirrors and winter candlelight set the scene for a loveable cast of wizened regulars, corner-seat scribes and melancholy dames. Watch the show with a soothing *öl* (beer) and a serve of soulful *husmanskost*. Try the traditional herring platter (Skr179). (☏08-32 25 18; www.tennstopet.se; Dalagatan 50; dagens Skr129; ☻11.30am-1am Mon-Fri, 1pm-1am Sat & Sun; Ⓜ Odenplan)

Storstad   FRENCH, SWEDISH $$$

 Map p114, D2

This attractive bistro near Odenplan, which shares a corner (and owners) with Olssons (p119) bar, serves Scandi classics like *toast skagen* (or Swedish meatballs alongside traditional French favourites like *moules-frites* and tarte

Understand
Stockholm Food & Drink

Sweden has come a long way from the days of all-beige fish and potato platters. Not only has immigration and membership in the EU introduced new flavours to the Swedish menu, a new wave of bold young chefs has been experimenting with traditional Swedish fare and melding it with various other influences. The result is an exciting dining scene on a par with some of the best food cities in Europe.

Classic Cuisine

Traditional Swedish cuisine is based on simple, everyday ingredients known generally as *husmanskost*, or basic home cooking. The most famous example of this, naturally, is Swedish meatballs. Other classic *husmanskost* dishes, largely based around fish and potatoes, include various forms of pickled and fried herring, cured salmon (gravlax), and *pytt i panna*, a potato hash served with sliced beets and a fried egg on top that may be the ultimate comfort food. Open-face shrimp sandwiches are everywhere, piled high with varying degrees of art and mayonnaise. Of course, the most thorough introduction to all the staples of Swedish cooking is the smörgåsbord, commonly available during the winter holidays.

Modern Menus

Essentially, contemporary Swedish cuisine melds global influences with local produce and innovation. Locals have rediscovered the virtues of their own pantry, alongside the more intense flavours arriving in Sweden from abroad. The result is a great passion for seasonal, home-grown ingredients, whether apples from Kivik or bleak roe from Kalix, used in creative new ways.

Equally important is the seasonality of food: expect succulent berries in spring, artichokes and crayfish in summer, and hearty truffles and root vegetables in the colder months. Alongside this appreciation for the cycles of farming has come a newfound reliance on sustainable, small-scale farmers and organic produce. Increasingly, restaurants and cafes pride themselves on serving organically grown and raised food, as well as actively supporting ethical, ecofriendly agricultural practices.

Swedish meatballs with potatoes and lingonberries

Tatin. It transforms into a lively cocktail bar later in the evening. (www.storstad.se; Odengatan 41; mains Skr165-275, herring plates Skr65-165; ⊗4pm-1am Mon-Wed, to 3am Fri & Sat; MOdenplan)

Drinking

Olssons   BAR

12 ⊙ Map p114, D2

The blue neon sign outside this bar tips you off to its former life as a shoe store. These days, it serves as the back bar to Storstad (p117), forming a busy corner of activity along this neigh-bourhoody street. (☎08-673 38 00; Odengatan 41; ⊗9pm-3am Wed-Sat)

Top Sights
Stockholm Archipelago

Getting There

The gateway to the archipelago, Vaxholm, is 35km northeast of Stockholm.

⚓ Waxholmsbolaget (www.waxholmsbola-get.se) is the main traffic provider; single trip costs Skr45 to Skr130.

Mention the archipelago to Stockholmers and prepare for gushing adulation. Buffering the city from the open Baltic Sea, it's a mesmerising wonderland of rocky isles carpeted with deep forests and fields of wildflowers, dotted with yachts and little red wooden cottages.

Exactly how many islands there are is debatable, with headcounts ranging from 14,000 to 100,000 (the general consensus is 24,000). It's an unmissable area and much closer to the city than many visitors imagine, with regular ferry services and various organised tours.

Don't Miss

Vaxholm

Vaxholm is the capital of and gateway to the archipelago, and it's a charming village, though its proximity to Stockholm (just a quick bus ride) means it can be crowded in summer. Still, on a sunny spring day, its crooked streets and storybook houses are irresistible. It has a thriving restaurant scene – headed by the landmark **Waxholms Hotell** (☎08-54 13 01 50; www.waxholmshotell.se; Hamngatan 2; lunch Skr105, mains Skr159-355; ☉noon-10.30pm, to 9pm Sun) – and a popular Christmas market. For pastries, try Vaxholms Bakery.

Utö

Star of the archipelago's southern section, Utö has it all: sublime sandy beaches, lush fairy-tale forests, sleepy farms, abundant bird life, an awesome organic bakery, **Utö Bageri** (breakfast Skr80-120, lunch Skr140, sandwiches Skr40-70; ☉8am-5pm), and a highly rated restaurant, **Nya Dannekrogen** (☎08-50 15 70 79; www.nyadannekrogen.se; Bygatan 1; mains Skr150-250; ☉May-Sep). Dining and accommodation are in Gruvbryggan, the island's northernmost village and its main ferry stop. Utö's network of roads and tracks make for heavenly cycling sessions; ask at the guest harbour about cycle hire.

Arholma

Arholma is a quiet, idyllic island in the archipelago's far north. Practically everything here was burnt down during a Russian invasion in 1719. The landmark lighthouse was rebuilt in the 19th century and is now an art gallery with impressive views. A popular resort in the early 20th-century, Arholma has a moneyed yet agricultural feel,

☑ Top Tips

▶ The Waxholmsbolaget ferry company divides the archipelago into three sections: middle, north and south. Within each section, several numbered routes go out and back, usually once a day, calling at various ports along the way. Think of them as rural bus routes, but on water.

▶ Keep in mind that most of the island villages are very remote, with limited options for dining and groceries; bring some provisions along. There are also bar-restaurants on the boats.

✗ Take a Break

You're likely to end up in Vaxholm on any archipelago journey, either to change ferries or just strolling around to enjoy the pretty harbour town. While you're here, head to the historic Waxholms Hotell for a scrumptious seafood meal.

Understand
Fast or Slow?

There are essentially two ways to visit the archipelago, depending on your preferred travel style:

▶ If time is short, take an organised boat tour of anywhere from a few hours to a full day, passing several islands and making brief stops at one or two. Check with **Stromma Kanalbolaget** (☎08-12 00 40 00; www.stromma.se; Strandvägen 8) for options that suit you – the most thorough option is the popular 'Thousand Islands' tour (from Skr1150), which includes lunch and dinner and takes in parts of the outer archipelago.

▶ Otherwise, you can plan your own longer, slower, self-guided trip using **Waxholmsbolaget** (☎08-679 58 30; www.waxholmsbolaget.se; Strömkajen; single trip Skr45-130, 5-/30-day pass Skr440/770; ☺8am-6pm; ⓜKungsträdgården) services with overnight stays. The area's many comfortable hostels, campsites and cushy hotels – plus some excellent restaurants – make the latter option dreamy if you have a few days to spare, though it does take a bit more planning.

with pastures, walking trails and fine sandy beaches, plus the excellent **Bull-August Vandrarhem** (☎0176-560 18; www.bullaugust.se; Arholma Södra Byväg 8; s/d from Skr340/575) hostel.

Finnhamn

This 900m-long island, northeast of Stockholm, combines lush woods and meadows with sheltered coves, rocky cliffs and visiting eagle owls. It's a popular summertime spot, but there are enough quiet corners to indulge your inner hermit. Walking trails cover most of the island, taking in awesome panoramic views at various points. Don't miss out on the top-notch restaurant, **Finnhamns Krog** (☎08-54 24 62 12; www.finnhamn. se; Ingmarsö; starters Skr98-185, mains Skr175-265; ☺11am-9pm Jun-Aug, weekends only rest of year), known for stellar versions of regional specialities and seafood.

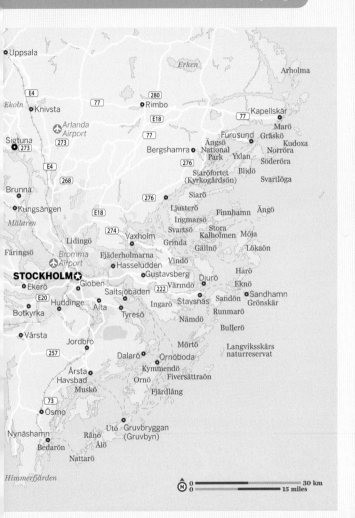

The Best of
Stockholm

Sergels Torg, Norrmalm
NICHOLAS PITT / GETTY IMAGES ©

Best Walks
Gamla Stan & Around

🏃 The Walk

Gamla Stan transports you back in time to Stockholm's early history. Most of the tourist activity is concentrated on Västerlånggatan and Stora Nygatan, but if you venture into the back alleys and quieter, crookeder streets, you'll find a city that seems almost unchanged since medieval times.

Start Ⓜ Gamla Stan

Finish Ⓜ Gamla Stan

Length 2.5km; 1½ hours

✗ Take a Break

Stop in at the casual **Cafe Järntorget** (Västerlånggatan 81; ice cream Skr27-78; ☺8am-6pm Mon-Fri, 10am-6pm Sat & Sun, open late in summer; Ⓜ Gamla Stan) for a scoop or two (you'll want at least two) of the most eccentrically Swedish ice-cream flavours you'll ever find, from saffron and honey to black licorice.

Cafe in Gamla Stan

PETER FORSBERG / ALAMY ©

❶ Riddarholmen

Other than its lovely **cathedral** (p31), this undervisited islet doesn't have a lot in the way of tourist activity, but it's extremely pretty to wander around, with its cobblestone streets and compressed huddle of fairy-tale buildings in delicate pastel shades.

❷ Evert Taubes Terrass

At the far west side of Riddarholmen is this flat terrace covered with tiny paving stones and decorated by impressive sculptures at either end. The singing lute player, *Everlife,* portrays the terrace's namesake, Swedish troubadour Evert Taube, in a 1990 bronze by Willy Gordon. The sculpture at the opposite end is *Solbåten* (1966), by Christian Berg.

❸ Riddarhuset

Heading back toward Gamla Stan, you'll pass Riddarhuset, a big pink-and-turquoise building that slightly resembles a wedding cake. This is the House of Nobility (or House of Knights), designed by French father-son architects Simon and Jean de la Vallée and completed in 1660. The statue in front is Axel Oxenstierna (1583–1654), a close adviser to Queen Christina.

4 Stortorget

Make your way to Mynttorget and turn down Västerlånggatan, the main shopping street, for a few blocks, then zigzag up to quieter Prästgatan. Turn left up the hill to Stortorget, the old town's beautiful main square. It's lined with gorgeous old buildings and usually

filled with happy holidaymakers; you'd never know it was once the scene of a massacre (the Stockholm Bloodbath of 1520).

5 Köpmantorget

Stroll down Köpmangatan ('Merchant's Street') to the triangular 'square' at its end, where you'll find a 1912 bronze replica of Berndt Notke's wooden statue from the 1400s, *St George and the Dragon,* which occupies **Storkyrkan** (p30). Take the road that slopes off to the right,

and continue along Österlånggatan, another major commercial thoroughfare.

6 Järntorget

At the end of Österlånggatan is this pretty square, barely younger than Stortorget (it dates to 1300). It began as an important trade spot, first for corn, then iron. As you continue back toward the starting point, peek up Mårten Trötzigs gränd – the narrowest street in town, which squiggles off to the right from Västerlånggatan.

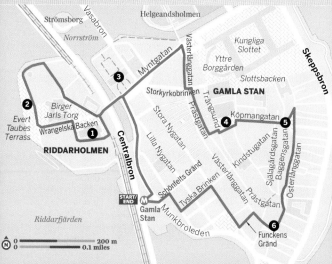

Best Walks
Water's Edge Walk

🏃 The Walk

It's not for nothing Stockholm calls itself 'Beauty on Water.' The city is built across 14 islands and has miles of waterfront. This walk takes you along some of the best bits, with maximum postcard potential and a few key places to stop. It's best to do it in the late afternoon or early evening, and don't forget to bring a camera.

Start Ⓜ Slussen

Finish Kastellholmen

Length 8km; one to three hours

🍴 Take a Break

For a quick snack that couldn't possibly be more typically Swedish, grab a herring plate from the **Nystekt Strömming** (Södermalmstorg; combo plates Skr35-75; 🕙11am-8pm Mon-Fri, to 6pm Sat & Sun, closing times vary) cart outside the Slussen tunnelbana stop. There's a picnic table nearby for resting your legs.

Skeppsholmsbron

JÖRG GREUEL / GETTY IMAGES ©

❶ Monteliusvägen

Follow Hornsgatan west from the Slussen tunnelbana stop; you'll pass **Akkurat** (p80), noteworthy as an excellent place to find good beer in Stockholm. Turn right at Bellmansgatan, then left at Bastugatan, which leads you to the tiny footpath called Monteliusvägen. This path extends through historic houses on one side, and on the other offers amazing views across the water and over the town.

❷ Fjällgatan

Cross back over the Slussen area and take Katarinavägen up the hillside, until it connects with Fjällgatan. This tiny street is the twin of Monteliusvägen – a gravel track through antique houses, it provides astounding views over the city from a slightly different angle. At its start/end point near **Hermans Trädgårdscafé** (p76) there's a rickety set of stairs leading down to the ground-level street, Stadsgårdsleden. Follow this back toward Slussen.

3 Skeppsbrokajen

Stay next to the water as you walk across Gamla Stan, following Skeppsbron and Skeppsbrokajen. You'll see lots of boat traffic through here, and there's an uninterrupted view across the water (Strömmen) of Skeppsholmen.

4 Strömparterren

Round the corner by the **palace** (p24) and turn right to walk across Norrbro. This small bridge, which crosses the sculpted park area known as Strömparterren, was nearly demolished to make way for a parking lot. Instead, thanks to some important underground discoveries, it now houses the excellent **Medeltidsmuseet** (p30). Follow the bridge and turn right, keeping to the water's edge as you walk alongside Norrström and onto the footbridge to Skeppsholmen.

5 Kastellet

Walk along the westernmost edge of the parklike Skeppsholmen, passing by the famous floating youth hostel Vandrarhem af Chapman & Skeppsholmen. At the far end of the island is an even smaller islet, called Kastellholmen, where there's a fortress called Kastellet. Circle the edge of the islet for what is essentially a 360-degree, panoramic view of the surrounding areas, including Gamla Stan, Södermalm and Djurgården.

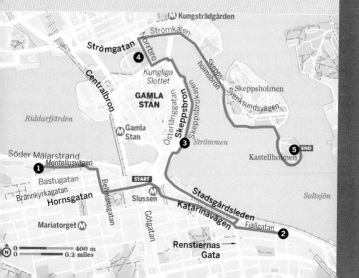

Best
Eating

Stockholm takes its dining seriously: the city has 11 Michelin stars to its name. This is excellent news for food-focused visitors. Whether you're after ultra-traditional Swedish favourites – like meatballs with lingonberry sauce, fried Baltic herring or an elaborately stacked shrimp sandwich – or more interested in the experimental, modern side, you're in luck.

Street Snacks

In the world of Swedish street food, hot dogs reign supreme – the basic model is called a *grillad korv med bröd* (hot dog in a bun), although you can also ask for it boiled *(kokt)*. Adventurous souls can request a mind-boggling variety of things done to the *korv*, chiefly involving rolling it up in flatbread with accompaniments from shrimp salad to mashed potatoes.

Festive Flavours

Around Christmas, many restaurants start offering a *julbord*, a particularly gluttonous version of Sweden's world-famous smörgåsbord buffet. Among the usual delicacies of herring, gravlax, meatballs, short ribs and blood pudding are seasonal gems like *Janssons frestelse*, a casserole of sweet cream, potato, onion and anchovy.

Daily Lunch

The weekday lunch special called *dagens rätt* is the secret to eating well on a budget in Stockholm. Typically Skr85 to Skr125, it's usually a set menu served between 11am and 2pm Monday to Friday and includes a hot main dish, salad, drink, bread and coffee. It's a practice originally supported and subsidised by the Swedish government.

☑ **Top Tips**

▶ There's nearly always a vegetarian item – or several – on the menu at any Swedish restaurant.

▶ Many vegetarian eateries are also all-you-can-eat buffets, which are massively popular with locals.

▶ One seasonal treat is Arctic char, a cousin of salmon and trout. Called *röding* in Swedish, the mild-flavoured char is a chefs' favourite, acting as a blank canvas that can handle all kinds of interesting treatments.

Den Gyldene Freden

Best Restaurants

Tranan An upscale neighbourhood joint serving impeccable Swedish cuisine. (p116)

Kryp In Classy, unstuffy top-end place with sublime takes on traditional Swedish dishes. (p33)

Den Gyldene Freden Stockholm's oldest restaurant, a traditional mainstay. (p34)

Mälarpaviljongen Floating restaurant with excellent cocktails. (p103)

Mathias Dahlgren Celebrity chef showing his stuff. (p44)

Grands Verandan Best place for a smörgåsbord. (p43)

Lisa Elmqvist Premier seafood restaurant in Östermalms Saluhall. (p90)

Best for Vegetarians

Lao Wai All-vegan Asian eatery with a fantastic weekday lunch special. (p115)

Hermitage Excellent-value veggie buffet in the old town. (p33)

Vurma Casual neighbourhood cafe with great salads. (p103)

Rosendals Trädgårds-kafe Idyllic cafe in a botanical garden. (p67)

Chutney Great-value veggie lunch spot. (p77)

Best
Museums & Galleries

Stockholm does museums right – there's really not a bad one in the bunch. Maybe it's a perk of having a design-obsessed culture – whatever the reason, this city makes learning fun. Its art galleries are intensely stylish, the kind of places you want to dress up for, and its history museums employ multimedia to enthral you in new worlds.

Best Museums

Kungliga Slottet The royal palace contains a number of museums and is itself a masterpiece. (p24)

Skansen Open-air museum of Swedish history and culture. (p52)

Vasamuseet Purpose-built museum devoted to a sunken warship. (p56)

Historiska Museet Engrossing multimedia presentation of Sweden's history. (p84)

Nobelmuseet Get inspired by stories of the most creative minds of our time. (p30)

Medeltidsmuseet Visit medieval Stockholm and the underpinnings of the royal palace. (p30)

Nordiska Museet Swedish art and artefacts through the ages, entertainingly arranged. (p63)

Spritmuseum A fun look at the complicated relationship Sweden has with alcohol. (p63)

Tekniska Museet Kids of all ages will be fascinated by seeing how stuff works. (p95)

Etnografiska Museet Well-crafted displays bring other cultures to life. (p95)

Best Galleries

Moderna Museet One of the best places in Europe to see modern art. (p58)

Bonniers Konsthall Cutting-edge art in a cutting-edge building. (p115)

Prins Eugens Waldemarsudde An excellent gallery in a beautiful waterside location. (p64)

Best
Shopping

Shopping is a sport, a pleasure and an art form in Stockholm. Whether you're just browsing or looking for specific gifts to bring home, there are plenty of options spread across the various neighbourhoods. Don't forget that on most major purchases, depending on where you live, you can reclaim your sales tax at customs when departing the country.

LONELY PLANET / GETTY IMAGES ©

What to Look For

Quintessentially Swedish things to bring home as gifts and souvenirs include hand-carved wooden toys and figures, such as the famous painted Dalahäst figures; glass and crystal, both decorative and utilitarian; fine linens and textiles; and intricate Sami handicrafts, especially leather, woodwork and jewellery made of woven metal threads.

Where to Shop

For classic souvenirs, T-shirts and postcards, head to Drottninggatan in the city centre or to Västerlånggatan in Gamla Stan. For high-end boutiques, go to Norrmalm and Östermalm. For secondhand and quirkier items, try Södermalm.

NK Department store with high-end versions of just about everything. (p49)

Svensk Slöjd Top-quality Swedish handicrafts. (p93)

Svenskt Tenn The grandfather of forward-thinking Scandinavian design – practically a museum. (p93)

Acne Jeans and high-style fashions. (p38)

Marimekko Bright, fun patterns in an inviting shopfront. (p38)

Science Fiction Bookshop Fun place to find games and books in English or Swedish. (p35)

Studio Lena M Adorable versions of traditional Swedish textiles, prints and decorative items. (p35)

Best
Design

Stockholm is all about good design, merging form and function in a relatively democratic – or at least ubiquitous – way. Whether you're hoping to bring samples of it back home with you, be inspired by how it's used, or just admire Scandi style in its native environment, there's no shortage of places to seek it out.

Furniture

Sweden may not have invented the squared circle but it has certainly embraced it. Spartan furnishings are characteristic of Scandinavia, and the furnishings you do find are usually the picture of elegant restraint, all clean lines and natural materials. Check out antiques as well as ultra-modern design shops to see how styles have – and have not – changed over the years.

Fabrics

One of the trademarks of Scandinavian design, and an early medium for experimentation with colour and graphics, is found in the realm of textiles. Patterned fabric on furniture, in windows, as wall hangings, or shaped into handbags or jackets, hats or dresses or even lampshades, is one of the most prominent embodiments of typical Swedish design.

The Whole Package

The best way to gain an appreciation for Swedish design is to see it as it was intended, in its native habitat. There are several well-known 'design hotels' in the city, including the Birger Jarl (p49), one of the earliest examples. And practically every restaurant or bar we list in this book has a noteworthy design, whether traditional or modern and edgy. Swoop in, admire, take notes if you like – after all, good design is meant for everyone.

Svenskt Tenn A great place to see traditional Scandinavian design. (p93)

Nordiska Galleriet A vast showroom for edgy furnishings, like IKEA-plus. (p93)

Nordiska Museet Huge collection of design objects from the history of Scandinavian design. (p63)

Café Opera Glitzy venue revamped by Thomas Sandell. (p48)

Sturehof Popular high-end seafood restaurant and chic bar designed by Jonas Bohlin. (p91)

Best
Coffee Shops

TIME E WHITE / ALAMY ©

Coffee is integral to Swedish life, to the point that meeting friends for a coffee break has its own verb: *fika*. Swedes drink more coffee than people in any other country except Finland. The range of coffee drinks has vastly increased in recent years, as has the variety of places to enjoy them. Don't forget to include a sweet – Stockholm does some heavenly cakes and pastries.

Xoko Responsible for baking the desserts served at the Nobel banquet each year. (p116)

Caffé Nero Almost aggressively cool coffee shop that also serves substantial meals. (p116)

Sturekatten A rickety labyrinth of tea tables and cosy corners

with old-auntie decor. (p91)

Café Saturnus Known for its massive cinnamon buns, pretty decor and excellent staff. (p91)

Grillska Husets Konditori Awesome bakery with outdoor seating on Gamla Stan's historic main square. (p34)

Vetekatten Fabulous sandwiches and pastries in a sprawling yet cosy space. (p45)

String Mismatched decor and casual vibe pulls in a cool crowd. (p78)

Best
Nightlife

Nightlife in Stockholm ranges from a quiet pint in an underground cellar to a neon-lit disco that only gets kicking around 3am. If you're just aiming to grab a beer in a pub, even a nice one, no special arrangements are required. But if you plan to hit the late-night clubs, you'll want to pre-pare. If possible, check the website to see if you can add yourself to the guest list – this is especially useful if you're on a tight schedule or only have one night to go clubbing and don't want to risk being shut out. Dress your best, bring loads of cash and follow your instincts – or follow the crowd – and you're bound to find a good time.

☑ Top Tips

▶ Coat checks are mandatory in many clubs and bars. There's usually a small fee (Skr20 to Skr30).

▶ On popular nights, clubs may also charge a fairly hefty admission fee (Skr150 to Skr200) – and make you wait in line. To better your odds, visit the club's website ahead of time to see if it offers a guest list.

▶ Some clubs stay open later than the tunnelbana runs. Budget for a taxi.

Pet Sounds Bar
Indie-rock hang-out with a great happy hour. (p79)

Monks Porter House
Dark cellar with a list that's a dream come true for beer nerds. (p35)

Le Rouge Decadent and sexy Gamla Stan lounge. (p35)

Absolut Icebar Touristy but irresistible – bundle up and sip frosty drinks in a bar made of ice. (p45)

Akkurat A great beer hall with a vast selection and a comfy covered patio. (p80)

Berns Salonger A Stockholm institution and glitzy dance club in historic environs. (p45)

Lilla Baren at Riche Very pretty bar for a slightly older, calmer set. (p92)

Spy Bar Famously difficult to get into, unless you're famous (or look it). (p92)

Laroy A crowded night-club below Spy Bar. (p92)

Sturecompagniet The Östermalm disco most likely to be rec-ommended by actual Stockholm residents. (p92)

Best
For Kids

Stockholm is a great place to travel with kids – there's plenty to do to keep them entertained, and the city's transport and infrastructure are set up for ease of use. On top of that, many museums offer free admission to children under 18 (sometimes older). Most attractions have kid-friendly areas and activities, but these are especially geared toward younger travellers.

RACHEL LEWIS / GETTY IMAGES ©

Junibacken Spend some time with Pippi Long-stocking and her pals in Astrid Lindgren's world. (p64)

Aquaria Vattenmu-seum Though it has an educational message, this place is also just fun to wander through. (p64)

Gröna Lund Tivoli Theme park with games, rides and roller coasters. (p65)

Spårvägsmuseet Play tunnelbana driver and see how the excellent Stockholm transit system came to be. (p76)

Leksaksmuseet Toys of all kinds cram the shelves at this out-of-the-way museum. (p76)

Skansen Obvious top choice for family fun, with a zoo and dozens of activities. (p52)

Best
For Free

Check museum schedules for free nights –
most of them offer one or two a week. Several
of the best museums in Stockholm offer free
admission to children (usually meaning anyone
under age 18, sometimes up to 20). Public parks
and beaches are also good free activities, as is
window-shopping, people-watching or wandering through park-laden neighbourhoods like
Djurgården or Gärdet.

Stadshuset Swimming
here is free if you're bold
enough to join the locals
diving from the City Hall
terrace. (p100)

Rålambshovsparken
Swim, play, picnic or just
hang out in this large
park. (p107)

Moderna Museet From
6pm to 8pm Fridays, see
world-class art and save
big on the admission fee.
(p58)

Stampen Join a fun,
lively crowd of mostly
regulars at the 2pm
Saturday blues jam.
(p34)

Tekniska Museet From
5pm to 8pm Wednesday,
bring the whole family
in to roam this huge, fun
museum. (p95)

Kulturhuset Plenty
of free kids' activities
here, from crafts to a
comic-book library.
(p43)

Best
Architecture

Stockholm has an impressive selection of buildings preserved from various important eras of architecture, including several by the Tessins, the father-son architect team that shaped much of the city's current appearance. For a good overview of Swedish architecture and its various lineages, as well as quick primers on current movements, stop in at Arkitektur- och Designcentrum (p66), the next-door neighbour to Moderna Museet.

Early Styles

Most of Stockholm's notable buildings are pre-modernist – the two royal palaces, Kungliga Slottet and Drottningholm, for example, and the imposing Stadshuset. A fairly brief but noteworthy period in regional architecture was Swedish National Romanticism – an often decorative classical free-style with Arts and Crafts influences, also known as Jugendstil.

Names to Drop

Gunnar Asplund (1885–1940) is arguably Sweden's most important modern architect. He's responsible for the iconic Stadsbiblioteket as well as the stunning Skogskyrkogården cemetery. Another name you'll hear frequently is Peter Celsing, who designed the stubbornly contemporary Kulturhuset.

Many of the most important buildings in Stockholm were designed by the court architect Nicodemus Tessin the Elder. Tessin the Younger designed the 'new' Kungliga Slottet and worked on several other standout buildings.

DESIGNED BY BERG ARCHITECTS / JOHNÉR / GETTY IMAGES ©

Stadsbiblioteket A graceful building, any way you look at it. (p115)

Kulturhuset Determined to push the envelope, even when unpopular. (p43)

Dramaten The Royal Dramatic Theatre is a decadent example of Jugendstil glory. (p92)

Stadshuset The City Hall is sturdy and square on the outside, secretly glittering within. (p100)

Östermalms Saluhall A cathedral of gourmet food, delectable both inside and out. (p91)

Globen The giant white golf ball at the southern tip of the city. (p81)

Best
Music

There's a greater variety of Swedish music than one might realise from listening to the public airwaves. Jazz and blues are huge here, classical concerts can be surprisingly affordable, and big names in rock and pop music tour through the city regularly. Look for posters tacked up around town advertising marquee shows.

Jazz

Swedish jazz has been going strong since the 1930s, and peaked in the '50s with artists such as Lars Gullin and Monica Zetterlund. Live jazz clubs are popular, and if you're a fan, the annual Stockholm Jazz Festival (p142) is not to be missed.

Rock & Pop

Everyone knows about ABBA of course, and fans can check out their museum (p64), but that's only the beginning of the Swedish influence over global pop music. Sweden is the third-largest exporter of music in the world, behind the US and UK, remarkable when you consider the size of the population.

Opera, Classical & Dance

There's no shortage of live-performance experiences in this realm, either. The Stockholm Opera's building is a national landmark and hard to miss. Dansens Hus offers a vibrant, up-to-date program, and the concert series at Konserthuset is both affordable and accessible.

Mosebacke Etablissement Big-name live bands as well as local faves perform here. (p81)

Best Jazz Venues

Stampen Homey jazz joint in Gamla Stan. (p34)

Fasching The premier jazz club in Stockholm. (p47)

Best Opera, Classical & Dance

Dansens Hus If you prefer a bit of movement with your music – a can't-miss for dance fans. (p47)

Konserthuset Classical concerts are held in this elegant blue building. (p47)

Operan The royal opera house – any visit here is an experience. (p47)

Best Live Venues

Glenn Miller Café Friendly neighbourhood blues bar with a casual vibe. (p47)

Debaser For indie rock and mainstream live acts, check out this venue on Medborgarplatsen. (p80)

Best
LGBT

Stockholm doesn't really have a queer district as such – gays and lesbians fit into the warm and welcoming mainstream so well that there's little need for one. Gay bars and clubs are scattered across the city, but even at nominally gay venues, crowds tend to be a mix of gay and straight, and places are generally open to anyone. Same-sex couples get hitched and have kids, and the government is vigilant about preventing discrimination.

Resources

For pretty extensive club listings, check out *QX* (www.qx.se), a magazine and website devoted to Stockholm's gay and lesbian nightlife. Tourist offices also produce a *Gay Stockholm* map. Since the hottest venues and party spots change regularly, be sure to ask around for the latest. And if your schedule allows, visit during Stockholm Pride (p142), in late July or early August, a weeklong party and Scandinavia's biggest pride week.

Best LGBT Eateries

Chokladkoppen Excellent place to get a latte and scope the Stockholm eye candy. (p34)

Mälarpaviljongen Killer cocktails and good food in a beautiful, gay-friendly waterside venue. (p103)

Best LGBT Nightlife

Torget Comfy, classy little spot in Gamla Stan. (p35)

Lady Patricia Party boat that welcomes all. (p80)

Best
Festivals & Events

CHRISTIAN ASLUND / GETTY IMAGES ©

There's nearly always something going on in Stockholm, especially during the summer months. Whether you're interested in grazing the offerings of some of the city's best restaurants, sampling some international music or film, or just exploring whatever's on the seasonal activity menu, you're likely to find something of interest. Check out Kungsträdgården, in the city centre, for weekend activities, or ask what's on at the tourist office.

Stockholm International Film Festival (www.stockholmfilmfestival.se) Held in November, this is a major celebration of local and international cinema whose guest speakers include top actors and directors.

Smaka På Stockholm (www.smakapastockholm.se) A five-day celebration of the Stockholm area's food scene held in late May/early June. The program includes gourmet food stalls (including representatives from several archipelago restaurants) and entertainment on Kungsträdgården.

Stockholm Pride (www.stockholmpride.org) In late July/early August Stockholm goes pink with a week of parties and cultural events plus a pride parade.

Stockholm Jazz Festival (www.stockholmjazz.com) One of Europe's premier jazz festivals, held in October and headquartered at Fasching.

Best
Fashion

Stockholm is Sweden's fashion hub, a major producer and exporter of emerging design talent. The big shopping districts are also home to just about every imaginable international design name, from Stella McCartney to Louis Vuitton. There are also fabulous secondhand shops everywhere.

Sustainability

Perhaps unsurprisingly in a country as green as Sweden, sustainability is a big issue in fashion. Historically, the industry could be extremely harsh on the environment and has not always been known for sound labour practices. Several Swedish brands place an emphasis on keeping their manufacturing processes ecofriendly. For more about sustainability in fashion, take a look at the **Sustainable Fashion Academy** (www.sustainable-fashionacademy.org).

Acne Skinny jeans and impeccable cool, now world-famous and highly sought-after. (p38)

Marimekko Wild, playful patterns on everything from frocks to handbags and kitchen gadgets. (p38)

Filippa K Dead-serious design for grown-ups, and possibly the inventor of skinny jeans. (p39)

Whyred Understated and street-smart clothing inspired by musicians. (p39)

BLK DNM A new venture from the sketchbook of J Lindeberg. (p39)

Fifth Avenue Shoe Repair Cutting-edge clothing from an up-and-coming collective. (p39)

PETER FORSSBERG / ALAMY ©

☑ Top Tips

▶ **The Wall** (www.elin-kling.com/the-wall) Elin Kling's well-known site.

▶ **Stockholm Street Style** (www.stockholm-street-style.com) Street fashion blog.

▶ **Stockholm Fashion Week** (www.stockholmfashion-week.com) Held in autumn.

WESC Skater-inspired fashion and gear, marketed worldwide by the rich and famous. (p39)

Best
Parks

Beautiful parks are a dime a dozen in Stockholm; you can hardly turn a corner without finding one. Most have good places for a picnic, shade trees, nice benches and sturdy playground equipment for kids. Some also have lakes or beaches for swimming, good hiking trails and sometimes even small cafes for refreshments. Make like the locals and enjoy!

Picnics

Many of Stockholm's casual cafes and coffee shops will offer breakfast or lunch 'packets' which make excellent-value picnic fixings. You can also pick up supplies in the prepared food section of many supermarkets, or in department stores such as NK (p49), whose high-end grocery section has the makings of a luxurious picnic.

Beaches

You're allowed to swim from just about any place in Stockholm where you can elbow your way into the water, but some swimming areas are nicer than others. Ask around – lots of locals have secret favourites among the city's beaches – or head to the water's edge near Rålambshovsparken.

Royal Parks

Some of the city's parks have a royal lineage, notably Djurgården, both established and administered by various Swedish kings. Despite their highbrow pedigrees, they are open to the public and are excellent places to find good running, walking or cycling trails. And don't worry, you're very unlikely to encounter the king on a deer hunt here these days.

RACHEL LEWIS / GETTY IMAGES ©

Djurgården The historical home of the royal game park, established in the 15th century. (p50)

Observatorielunden A quiet, leafy escape from the city. (p116)

Vasaparken Lovely oasis in the middle of Vasastan. (p116)

Humlegården Home of the royal library and a peaceful hang-out in its own right. (p86)

Rålambshovsparken This park abuts an excellent public swimming beach. (p107)

Survival Guide

Survival Guide

Before You Go

When to Go

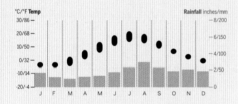

→ High Season (mid-Jun–Aug) Season starts at Midsummer; expect warm weather and most sights to be open, though some shops and restaurants take a few weeks' summer holiday. Hotel rates drop.

→ Shoulder (Sep-Oct) Weather is usually still good, even if there's no one else around to enjoy it. Hotel rates return to normal.

→ Low Season (Nov-May) Stockholm and its surrounds become a winter wonderland, with ice skating, skiing and heartwarming holiday markets. Most campsites and some hostels are closed.

Book Your Stay

☑ **Top Tip** Most hotels offer steep discounts in summer, on weekends and when booked in advance online.

→ Hotel prices usually include a large buffet breakfast.

→ Wi-fi is nearly always available and generally free

→ Parking usually comes with a fee (Skr150 to Skr250).

→ Central Stockholm hotel rooms can be very tiny, especially the budget rooms in midrange hotels.

Useful Websites

Guestroom B&B (www.gastrummet.com) A range of accommodation in apartments and B&Bs.

STF (www.svenskaturist foreningen.se) The main hostelling network.

Lonely Planet (www.lonelyplanet.com) Author-reviewed accommodation and online booking.

est Budget

ity Backpackers (www.
tybackpackers.org)
andy to Centralsta-
onen, this friendly hostel
as excellent facilities.

TF Fridhemsplan (www.
dhemsplan.se) Modern
ostel with great facilities,
otel-style rooms and
ool lounge areas.

**andrarhem af Chap-
an & Skeppsholmen**
ww.stfchapman.com)
eep on a historic con-
erted ship, or in dorms
the mainland.

est Midrange

otel Anno 1647 (www.
nno1647.se) Historic
otel off Södermalm's
ain thoroughfare, with
etty rooms and a nice
eakfast buffet.

otel Hansson (www.ho-
hansson.se) Family-run
outique hotel with
gh-design interiors and
epic breakfast buffet.

otel Hellsten (www.
llsten.se) Owned by an
thropologist, this cool
otel is decorated with
scinating found objects.

ordic 'C' Hotel (www.
ordicchotel.com) Sleek
oms and great service,

plus the Absolut Icebar
and nearby Arlanda
Express.

Best Top End

Grand Hôtel Stockholm
(www.grandhotel.se)
Where the literati, glitterati
and nobility call it a night.

Rival Hotel (www.rival.
se) Owned by ABBA's
Benny Andersson, this
lovely Mariatorget hotel is
1940s-cinema themed.

Berns Hotel (www.berns.
se) Ultra-stylish rooms
in fab location with top
entertainment systems.

Arriving in Stockholm

☑ **Top Tip** For the best
way to get to your accom-
modation, see p17.

Stockholm Arlanda Airport

➡ **Arlanda Express** (www.
arlandaexpress.com; one-way
Skr260) train service from
the airport to Centralstationen takes 20 minutes;
trains run every 10 to
15 minutes from about

5am to 12.30am (less
frequently after 9pm). In
peak summer season, two
adults can travel together
for Skr280 (one-way).

➡ **Flygbuss** (www.flygbuss-
arna.se) bus service from
the airport to city centre
runs every 10 or 15 min-
utes (Skr119, 50 minutes)
from stop 11 in Terminal
5. There are self-service
ticket kiosks throughout
the airport.

➡ Taxi services to or from
the airport cost about
Skr520 and take around
45 minutes.

Getting Around

Check out the trip plan-
ner at http://reseplan-
erare.resrobot.se.

Bicycle

☑ **Best for...** Exploring
Djurgården or taking bike
paths further afield.

➡ Bicycles can be carried
on SL local trains as fold-
able 'hand luggage' only.

➡ Bicycles are not allowed
in Centralstationen or on
the tunnelbana.

→ **Stockholm City Bikes** (www.citybikes.se) offers self-service bike-hire stands across the city. Bikes can be borrowed for three-hour stretches and returned at any stand. Purchase a card online or from the tourist office; a three-day card is Skr165, and a season pass (April–October) is Skr300.

Boat

☑ **Best for...** Scenic jaunts between neighbourhoods.

→ Djurgårdsfärjan city ferries serve Djurgården (summer only) and Slussen (year-round) about every 10 minutes. SL passes are valid.

→ For info on archipelago boats, see p122.

Bus

☑ **Best for...** Reaching the suburbs and sights not well served by the tunnelbana.

→ Ask at any SL or tourist office for the handy inner-city route map *Innerstadsbussar*. It's also available online (www.sl.se).

→ Bus 47 runs from Sergels Torg to Djurgården.

→ Bus 69 goes from Centralstationen and Sergels Torg to the Ladugårdsgärdet museums and Kaknästornet.

Car & Motorcycle

☑ **Best for...** Getting out of town.

→ Car-hire offices are plentiful near Centralstationen and at Arlanda Airport.

→ Driving in central Stockholm is not recommended because of the many one-way streets, congested bridges and limited parking.

→ Djurgårdsvägen is closed near Skansen at night, on summer weekends and some holidays

Taxi

☑ **Best for...** Getting around late at night or to and from the airport.

→ Taxis are readily available but expensive, so check for a meter or arrange the fare first.

→ The flagfall is around Skr45, then Skr10 to Skr13 per kilometre.

→ At night, women travelling alone should ask about *tjejtaxa*, a discount rate offered by some operators.

Tickets & Passes

All tunnelbana (T or T-bana) trains, local trains and buses are run by Storstockholms Lokaltrafik (SL). Purchase tickets and passes at tunnelbana stations, Cityterminalen and Pressbyrån stores. Your best option is to load a refillable SL travel card (Skr20) with single-trip or unlimited-travel credit. Students and seniors pay half-price. Note that tickets cannot be bought on buses.

→ single trip Skr25–50

→ unlimited 24-hour pass Skr115

→ unlimited 72-hour pass Skr230

→ seven-day pass Skr300

Use one of the estab-
lished, reputable firms,
such as **Taxi Stock-
holm** (☎15 00 00; www.
taxistockholm.se), **Taxi 020**
(☎020-20 20 20; www.
taxi020.se) and **Taxi Kurir**
(☎0771-86 00 00; www.
taxikurir.se).

Tunnelbana
(Metro)

Best for... Quickly
moving around the city
centre.

The most useful mode
of transport in Stock-
holm, run by **Storstock-
holms Lokaltrafik** (SL;
☎08-600 10 00; www.sl.se;
Centralstationen, Sergels
Torg).

Tunnelbana lines
converge on T-Centralen,
connected by an under-
ground walkway to
Centralstationen (and
Cityterminalen, the main
bus station).

Tram

Best for... Visiting
museums in Djurgården.

The historic No 7 tram
and its ultra-modern
cousins) runs between
Norrmalmstorg and the
Djurgården attractions.

SL passes are valid.

Essential Information

Business Hours
☑ **Top Tip** Many
restaurants and some
shops close in July or
August as Swedes take
their own holidays.
Check ahead to avoid
disappointment.

These hours reflect
high season (mid-June
through August). Expect
more limited hours the
rest of the year. Reviews
in this guide don't list
business hours unless
they differ from these
standards.

→ **Banks** 9.30am to 5pm
Monday to Friday

→ **Bars** 11am or noon to
1am or 2am

→ **Government offices**
9am to 5pm Monday to
Friday

→ **Restaurants** lunch
11am to 2pm, dinner
5pm to 10pm, often
closed on Sundays and/
or Mondays

→ **Shops** 10am to 6pm
Monday to Friday, 10am
to 1pm Saturday

Electricity

230V/50Hz

Discount Cards

→ **Stockholm Card**
(www.visitstockholm.
com) Adult passes for
24/48/72/120 hours cost
Skr450/625/750/950;
accompanying children
pay Skr215/255/285/315.
Available from tourist
offices, museums, some
hotels or online. Entry to
80 attractions, travel on
SL's public transport network, sightseeing by boat
and some walking tours.

→ **Destination Stock-
holm** (☎08-663 00 80;
www.destination-stockholm.
com) SL transit, sightseeing tours and admission
to 75 attractions. Two-/

Money-Saving Tips

➡ Book hotels and domestic travel online in advance.

➡ Hotels are generally twice as expensive outside the short summer season (mid-June to August).

➡ Make lunch your main meal, as the locals do: look for *dagens rätt,* the daily lunch special, usually excellent value even at top-end restaurants (Skr85 to Skr125).

three-/four-day cards Skr695/845/1035 (half-price for ages six to 15). Purchase the card online and have it shipped to you or pick it up on arrival. The website also has a hotel booking engine with about 40 participating hotels, which can be added to your discount packet (many are located in the suburbs or outskirts of town).

Emergency
☎ 112

Public Holidays
☑ **Top Tip** If you're visiting Stockholm in high season, note that the Midsummer holiday brings life to a halt for three days, including many tourist services: transport service is reduced, most shops and tourist offices close, and you'll see signs that

say *stängt* (closed) on museums and attractions. Note that Midsommar-afton (Midsummer's Eve; late June), Julafton (Christmas Eve; 24 December) and Nyårsafton (New Year's Eve; 31 December), though not official holidays, are generally nonworking days for most of the population.

Nyårsdag (New Year's Day) 1 January

Trettondedag Jul (Epiphany) 6 January

Långfredag, Påsk, Annandag Påsk (Good Friday, Easter Sunday, Easter Monday) March/April

Första Maj (Labour Day) 1 May

Kristi Himmelsfärds dag (Ascension Day) May/June

Pingst, Annandag Pingst (Whit Sunday and

Monday) Late May or early June

Midsommardag (Midsummer's Day) Saturday between 19 and 25 June

Alla Helgons dag (All Saints' Day) Saturday, late October or early November

Juldag (Christmas Day) 25 December

Annandag Jul (Boxing Day) 26 December

Telephone
Public pay phones are scarce. Those that still exist take a prepaid card (available at newsstands), not coins.

Mobile Phones

➡ You can bring your mobile phone from home and buy a Swedish SIM card, which gives you a Swedish mobile number and avoids racking up roaming charges. Local SIM cards are readily available (around Skr95; you then load them with credit (at least Skr100).

➡ Your mobile may be locked onto your local network in your home country, so ask your home network for advice before going abroad; most will gladly unlock your phone for travel.

nternational & omestic Calls

nternational calls

ial ☎00 + country ode + local area code + elephone number.

alls to Sweden Dial

☎46 + area code (omit he first zero) + telephone umber.

omestic calls Area

ode required.

seful Numbers

irectory assis- ance (☎118, ☎119) nternational.

irectory assistance (☎118) Within Sweden.

mergency services (☎112)

oilets

lost museums and tour- t offices have free toilets. ut most public toilets ost Skr5 to Skr10, usually ayable by coin only.

ourist Information

tockholm Visitors enter (☎08-50 82 85 ; www.visitstockholm.com; ulturhuset, Sergels Torg ⊙9am-7pm Mon-Fri, to m winter, 9am-4pm Sat, am-4pm Sun; Ⓜ️T-Cen- alen) The main visitors entre sits in Kulturhuset Sergels Torg.

Visit Djurgården
(☎08-667 77 01; www.
visitdjurgarden.se; Djurgårdsvägen 2; ⊙9am-dusk)
With tourist information
specific to Djurgården,
this office at the edge of
the Djurgården bridge is
attached to **Sjöcaféet**
(☎08-660 57 57; www.sjoca-
feet.se; ⊙9am-9pm Apr-Sep;
🚲7), so you can grab a
bite as you plot your day.

Travellers with Disabilities

➡ Sweden is one of the
easiest countries to travel
around in a wheelchair.
Transport services have
adapted facilities, ranging
from trains to taxis –
contact the operator
in advance for the best
service.

➡ Public toilets and
most hotel rooms have
facilities for people with
disabilities; **Hotels in
Sweden** (www.hotel-
sinsweden.net) indicates
whether hotels have
adapted rooms.

➡ For further information,
contact **De Handikap-
pades Riksförbund**
(☎08-685 80 00; www.dhr.
se), the national associa-
tion for the disabled.

Visas

➡ Citizens of EU countries
can enter Sweden with
a passport or national
identification card and
stay indefinitely.

➡ Non-EU passport hold-
ers from Australia, New
Zealand, Canada and the
US can enter and stay in
Sweden without a visa for
up to 90 days.

➡ Citizens of South Africa
and many other African,
Asian and some Eastern
European countries re-
quire tourist visas for entry to Sweden. These are
only available in advance
from Swedish embas-
sies (allow two months);
there's a nonrefundable
application fee of €60 for
most applicants. Visas
are good for any 90 days
within a six-month period.

Dos & Don'ts

Shoes Be prepared to take off your shoes inside
the front door when visiting a Swedish home.

Formal occasions Wait for the host to welcome
you to the table before eating or drinking.

Language

Most Swedish sounds are similar to their English counterparts. One exception is *fh* (a breathy sound pronounced with rounded lips, like saying 'f' and 'w' at the same time), but with a little practice, you'll soon get it right. Note also that *ai* is pronounced as in 'aisle', *aw* as in 'saw', *air* as in 'hair', *eu* as the 'u' in 'nurse', *ew* as the 'ee' in 'see' with rounded lips, and *ey* as the 'e' in 'bet' but longer. Just read our pronunciation guides as if they were English and you'll be understood. The stressed syllables are indicated with italics.

Basics

Hello.
Hej. — hey

Goodbye.
Hej då. — hey daw

Yes.
Ja. — yaa

No.
Nej. — ney

Please.
Tack. — tak

Thank you (very much).
Tack (så mycket) — tak (saw *mew*·ke)

You're welcome.
Varsågod. — var·sha·*gohd*

Excuse me.
Ursäkta mig. — oor·*shek*·ta mey

Sorry.
Förlåt. — feur·*lawt*

How are you?
Hur mår du? — hoor mawr doo

Fine, thanks. And you?
Bra, tack. Och dig? — braa tak o dey

What's your name?
Vad heter du? — vaad *hey*·ter doo

My name is ...
Jag heter ... — yaa *hey*·ter ...

Do you speak English?
Talar du engelska? — taa·lar doo eng·el·sk

I don't understand.
Jag förstår inte. — yaa feur·*shtawr* in·t

Eating & Drinking

What would you recommend?
Vad skulle ni rekommendera?
vaad *sku*·le nee re·ko·men·*dey*·ra

Do you have vegetarian food?
Har ni vegetarisk mat?
har nee ve·ge·*taa*·risk maat

I'll have ...
Jag vill ha ... — yaa vil haa ...

Cheers!
Skål! — skawl

I'd like (the) ...
Jag skulle vilja ha ...
yaa *sku*·le *vil*·yav haa ...

  bill
  räkningen — *reyk*·ning·en

  drink list
  drickslistan — driks·lis·tan

  menu
  menyn — me·*newn*

Emergencies

Help!
Hjälp! — yelp

Go away!
Försvinn! — feur·*shvin*

ll ...!
ng ...!   ring ...

a doctor
efter en doktor ef·ter en dok·tor

the police
olisen poh·lee·sen

n lost.
g har gått vilse. yaa har got vil·se

n sick.
g är sjuk. yaa air fhook

here are the toilets?
r är toaletten? var air toh·aa·le·ten

ransport & Directions

here's the ...?
r ligger ...? var li·ger ...

bank
banken ban·ken

post office
osten pos·ten

tourist office
turistinformationen
too·rist·in·for ma·fhoh·nen

I like one ... (to Stockholm) please.
g skulle vilja ha en ... (till Stockholm).
·a sku·le vil·ya haa eyn ... (til stok·holm)

one-way ticket
enkelbiljett en·kel·bil·yet

return ticket
returbiljett re·toor·bil·yet

hat time does the train/bus leave?
är avgår tåget/bussen?
ir aav·gawr taw·get/bu·sen

an you stop here?
n du stanna här?
n doo sta·na hair

Shopping & Services
I'm looking for ...
Jag letar efter ... yaa ley·tar ef·ter ...

How much is it?
Hur mycket kostar det?
hoor mew·ke kos·tar de

Time & Numbers
What time is it?
Hur mycket är klockan?
hur mew·ke air klo·kan

It's (two) o'clock.
Klockan är (två). klo·kan air (tvaw)

in the morning
på förmiddagen paw feur·mi·daa·gen

in the afternoon
på eftermiddagen paw ef·ter·mi·daa·gen

yesterday
igår ee·gawr

tomorrow
imorgon ee·mor·ron

1	ett	et
2	två	tvaw
3	tre	trey
4	fyra	few·ra
5	fem	fem
6	sex	seks
7	sju	fhoo
8	åtta	o·ta
9	nio	nee·oh
10	tio	tee·oh
100	ett hundra	et hun·dra
1000	ett tusen	et too·sen

Behind the Scenes

Send Us Your Feedback

We love to hear from travellers – your comments help make our books better. We read every word, and we guarantee that your feedback goes straight to the authors. Visit **lonelyplanet.com/contact** to submit your updates and suggestions.

Note: We may edit, reproduce and incorporate your comments in Lonely Planet products such as guidebooks, websites and digital products, so let us know if you don't want your comments reproduced or your name acknowledged. For a copy of our privacy policy visit lonelyplanet.com/privacy.

Our Readers

Thanks to the travellers who used the last edition and wrote to us with helpful hints, useful advice and interesting anecdotes:

Amin Amirali, Luke Archer, Priscila Elias Annibal, Philipp Drachenberg, Richard Lemon, Poornima Menon, Brigitte Tenni, Billy White

Becky's Thanks

Thanks to my dad, Joel Ohlsen, an awesome travel buddy, who joined me for the best part of the trip (the Stockholm archipelago) and against his better judgment let me plan our whole itinerary. Thanks also to editor Gemma Graham, an absolute pleasure to work with, and to the SPP team for help above and beyond the call of duty. A whiskey-soda and a big hug to Travis Gardner for keeping the cat and tomato plants alive while I was away.

Acknowledgments

Cover photograph: Relaxing on Skeppsholmen, Maurizio Rellini/ SIME/4Corners

This Book

This 3rd edition of Lonely Planet's *Pocket Stockholm* was written by Becky Ohlsen. The previous edition was written by Cristian Bonetto. This guidebook was produced by the following:

Destination Editor Gemma Graham **Product Editor** Martine Power **Senior Cartographers** David Kemp, Valentina Kremenchutskaya **Book Designer** Jennifer Mullins **Assisting Editors** Justin Flynn, Monique Perrin, Gabrielle Stefanos **Cover Researcher** Naomi Parker

Thanks to Sasha Baskett, Elin Berglund, Penny Cordner, Brendan Dempsey, Ryan Evans, Larissa Frost, Wayne Murphy, Claire Naylor, Karyn Noble, Dianne Schallmeiner, Ellie Simpson, Lyahna Spencer, Angela Tinson, Lauren Wellicome, Tony Wheeler

See also separate subindexes for:

⊗ **Eating p157**
⊘ **Drinking p157**
✪ **Entertainment p158**
⊜ **Shopping p158**

ndex

Sights 000
Map Pages 000

Our Writer

Becky Ohlsen

Each time she returns to Stockholm, Becky discovers something new. This time it was the world's greatest cardamom bun, encountered at an organic bakery on a remote island in the Stockholm archipelago. A huge fan of Stockholm, Becky has spent enough time in the city to know where to find the no-fee public toilets but not quite enough to have absorbed any of its impressive fashion sense. Maybe next time. Though raised in the mountains of Colorado, Becky has been exploring Sweden since childhood, while visiting her grandparents and other relatives. She is easily bribed with ice-cold *snaps* or saffron ice cream. Read more about Becky at: https://auth.lonelyplanet.com/profiles/BeckyOhlsen.

Published by Lonely Planet Publications Pty Ltd
ABN 36 005 607 983
3rd edition – Apr 2015
ISBN 978 1 74179 958 3
© Lonely Planet 2015   Photographs © as indicated 2015
10 9 8 7 6 5 4
Printed in China